SCARS AND STILETTOS

Lisa,
All things are
possible!
Dana

SCARS AND STILETTOS

HARMONY DUST

MONARCH
BOOKS

Oxford, UK & Grand Rapids, Michigan, USA

Published in association with the literary agency of Alive Communications,
Inc., 7680 Goddard Street, Suite 200, Colorado Springs, CO 80920.
www.alivecommunications.com

First published by Monarch Books
an imprint of
Lion Hudson plc
Wilkinson House, Jordan Hill Road,
Oxford OX2 8DR, England
Email: monarch@lionhudson.com
www.lionhudson.com/monarch

ISBN (UK): 978-1-85424-906-7 (print)
ISBN (US): 978-0-8254-6309-9 (print)
ISBN: 978-0-85721-137-8 (epub)
ISBN: 978-0-85721-136-1 (Kindle)

First edition 2009

Acknowledgments
Unless otherwise stated, Scripture quotations are taken from the Holy Bible,
New International Version, © 1973, 1978, 1984 by the International Bible Society.
Used by permission of Hodder & Stoughton Ltd. All rights reserved.

A catalogue record for this book is available from the British Library.

Printed and bound in the United States, March 2014, LH30

Free

I dance because I am free
Because I am surefooted as a deer
I move swiftly, paying careful attention
To the music that leads me
Striving to maintain connected
Constantly deciphering the Composer's
Intentions when he wrote the song
I honor the moments that insist on stillness
For in stillness is truth.
In silence, I hear your voice
In love, I am in your presence
In light, I dance in your way.

Harmony Dust
February 1999

This book is dedicated to…
My beautiful daughter, Johnny Ella, for showing me
a new facet of God's love.
My God, Immanuel, for your ever-present love
and grace.

Contents

Acknowledgments

Thank you…

To my sweet, precious Johnny girl: thank you for being the *best* baby on the planet and for sleeping so good, so that mommy could finish this book.

To my family: thank you for releasing me to share my story. Mom: thank you for always teaching us that we can be world-changers. Daddy Russ: thank you for saying 'yes' to being a father to me, and for giving me Noah. Dad and Noah: you are true artists and have made my life more colorful. Daddy Bill: thank you for bringing me into this world.

Grandma Mary: your tenacious spirit, passion, and prayers will be alive for generations to come. So will your card-playing skills.

MaSyh: you were a voice of reason in one of the most insane times of my life, and I will always cherish our childhood in Venice together.

Melissa: where would I be without you and your beautiful family? You showed me how to be a good friend and to give generously. There was never a bus bench too far, or an hour too late to call. Thank you.

Auntie Krissi: thank you for showing me the partnership between grace and integrity, and loving me when I needed both. Lauryn: you are still and always have been my favorite cousin – and not just because you are my only cousin either! Your passion for life, and for God, are breath-taking.

Melody: carpet picnics for life! Your friendship has been

a steady stream of goodness. April: you are the big sister I never had but always wanted. You hold it down like nobody's business! A gourmet cook with 17 children, a Master's degree, a teaching career, book clubs and marriage groups... are you sure you aren't Superwoman? Ashley: your character is as stunning as your heart; I am so thankful for your eyes of faith and lips that speak truth. Tanya: if you had not been the fierce, compassionate, goofball that you are, I don't know where I would be today. Lindsay: thank you for always seeing the best in people, including me. You have a gift for drawing out potential. Emily: how can one girl embody both Orange County and Compton? You are a faithful friend, and an enigma.

Jeff: words cannot express what a significant role you have played in my life and in John's. You are a stellar human being. Your prayer, direction, support, listening ear, kindness, and love have impacted our lives in unfathomable ways. Philip and Holly: thank you for being so faithful with God's calling on your lives. You have been examples to me in every way. Because of your integrity and perseverance, we have an amazing, loving, passionate, dynamic, and solid church that we can call home. Dan and Michelle: thank you for your commitment to your own marriage, and also to ours.

The Treasures Team, past, present, and future: you truly are incredible reflections of God's love, and I can't imagine life without you. How awesome it is that we get to do this together!

To the Denver Foundation: your generosity has changed lives and equipped me to fulfill my dreams. The Book Ends Club: thank you for your insight, listening ears, and for helping me face the blank page. Sheila Weller: thank you for caring enough about my story to tell it. Rita Williams: for your gentle yet challenging guidance in writing this book. Jan Greenough: for your keen eye and shaping hands. Tony Collins and Beth Jusino: for believing in this manuscript and taking a chance on me.

To Jesus: my cup runneth over. Thank you for life, and life abundant. Father, Friend, Redeemer, Lover of my soul: you have restored my hope, set me free and made me new. Thank you.

Preface

I can remember driving to Las Vegas on January 8th, 2002. An idea birthed over Chinese food, several months earlier, now had us headed to Sin City in a rented van packed with displays, equipment, and my wife in the front seat. We would only have to come once, and that would put XXXchurch.com (a Christian anti-pornography website that aims to help those who struggle with pornography) on the map. We made the trip to Vegas to launch our website at the largest adult expo in the country, fully expecting to be kicked out once they realized what we were about. We hadn't even considered coming back the following year. After all, no one was talking about leaving jobs and pursuing XXXchurch full-time. Spend a few days in Vegas, come back home, and the website will just run itself.

Within a few days everything changed. Under-staffed, outsmarted, and under-financed, we knew we could never compete with the 70-billion-dollar-a-year sex industry. But then, we realized, we didn't have to compete; we just needed to show up.

Just show up. Jesus said to 'Go'. He never called us to play it safe. Where He goes, we're to follow.

The thing that blows me away about Harmony's story is that she showed back up. How easy would it be never to set foot in a strip club ever again? The pain, the memories, the past, were all right there, but she decided that this was not about her, but about the hundreds of women that remained in the clubs.

A friend of mine wrote a song and played it in church quite

a bit. It said, 'You have been changed to bring change.' I really think that this should not only sum up your life; it sums up Jesus' message quite well. You have been changed to bring change.

Like Harmony, we all have a choice. Play it safe, and stay far away from our former employees, or our family that does not know the Lord, or our past – or show up again, and bring with us change.

When I read this book I got a real insight into the love that Harmony has for these women. As you read about the clubs, the patrons, and the dancers, you are excited when you finally read that she has left that lifestyle. But I felt even more excitement when I realized that she is going back to bring change.

You will learn a lot. You will read things that will upset you, but I hope you'll also appreciate the simple message that Harmony passes on about Jesus: the fact that you are loved and you are welcomed. The change that has taken Harmony away from dancing, but back to the clubs, could only come from Jesus. He wants to change you so you can bring change.

Craig Gross
XXX Church

Foreword

At one time or another, we have all been victims of something – from the not-so-big-a-deal to the absolutely devastating. I have looked at pictures of me taken in the 1980s. What was I thinking? I was tricked by the fashion industry into thinking those leg warmers looked good! I have also been a victim of breast cancer.

Some of us have been victims of someone else's narrow mind.

Many of us have been the victim of some kind of discrimination: the color of our skin; the money, or lack of it, in our bank account; the wheelchair; the accent; our gender; blonde hair (after all, you can't have a brain).

And we all get to choose whether we stay a victim or not.

Harmony's is the story of a girl who courageously decided not to remain a victim. She was the victim of so much pain that it breaks my heart, and yet she chose to survive. She did whatever it took to survive. And then she made the very brave decision to move from just being a survivor to becoming an overcomer.

A victim is in the dark.

A survivor sees a light at the end of the tunnel and hangs on.

An overcomer becomes the light for someone else.

Harmony wrote her story so that you and your friends may get help to move out of whatever dark tunnel you find yourself in. I know her heart, and it is to see all of us live our lives in the very purpose for which we were created. I do want to warn you – once you start this book, you will not be able to put it down. You will laugh, you will cry, you will be encouraged, you will fall in love with God all over again... and you will want to get a copy for every person you know.

Holly Wagner
Author and founder of GodChicks

Prologue

The haze of dusk was a soft blanket over my green Honda Civic as I drove the familiar route to the Los Angeles Airport. How many times had I taken this freeway? This exit? On autopilot, I changed lanes smoothly and rounded the bend towards Century Boulevard. I was going in the same direction I had always gone, but I might as well have been in a parallel universe to the one I lived in six years before.

Driving down Century, I saw the sign in the distance. The words 'Live Live Nude Nudes' hung in muted, orange and red 1970s-style lettering. You'd think with all the razzle-dazzle strip clubs popping up everywhere, this one would wither and die and go back to being something more functional, as it was when it was a bowling alley. But it's still there. And so are the girls.

I wondered about my old co-workers. Had they moved on to other clubs, or other lives, or were they still there?

I remembered that life: the suffocating feeling of being trapped, with no end in sight; wanting the money, *needing* it, but wishing there were some other legal way to get it. The constant pressure to smile, and pretend you want nothing more than to fulfill every wish and fantasy of a stranger, when all you really want to do is lie around your apartment in sweat pants, watching mafia movies like *Goodfellas* and *Casino* – imagining you could live some other life.

I remembered, and all I could do was pray: that the women

behind those very walls, feeling as I once did, would have a real and true encounter with the loving, gracious, God of freedom and wonder that I have come to know. That they would discover the beauty that lies within them that is more precious than the rarest gem. That they would realize that the dreams of their youth and the passions of their hearts are important, and within reach.

The driver in front of me gently pressed his brakes, snapping me out of the trance I was in. I glanced in my rear view mirror, and saw that I had passed the Taco Bell parking lot I was planning to pull in to. Instead, I parked in a lot directly across the street from the club, turned my car off, and sat staring. There are girls in there right now, I thought.

What are you going to do? A voice whispered to my heart. What *could* I do? I felt as though I was outside a prison that had once held me captive. I was free, while there were still women feeling trapped inside. There was a stand-off: I was still, waiting for something to happen. For the other guy, for some other person, to come up with something: a solution; an idea; anything.

What are you going to do? What can I do? It's not like I can waltz up there and tell the bouncer I want to talk to the girls. Even if he did let me in, what on earth would I say?

What do you want to say?

I glanced to my left and discovered a stack of postcards from a recent women's conference I had attended. The woman pictured was facing away from the camera, looking confidently ahead. Her back was draped with strands of pearls. Tattooed across the warm brown skin of her shoulder blades were the words, 'Her value... far above rubies and pearls.'

That is what I wanted to say. That is exactly what I wanted

the women in that club to hear. Hands shaking, I grabbed the stack of postcards and began writing on the back of each one: 'I was just driving by and wanted to tell you that you are loved...'

What else? 'If you are ever interested in going to church, I know of a great one: www.oasisla.org. You are welcome there! Love, Harmony. PS: I used to work here too.'

When I first started dancing, even if I wanted to go to church, it would never have occurred to me that a church would have me. Still sitting in the car, my legs were heavy and stiff as I held the postcards in my hands. I wondered if I was doing the right thing. Would people think I was crazy for going back there?

I approached the parking lot and there, scattered between orange cones, were the dancers' cars. 'My' spot was among them. Each night, when the security saw my car pulling into the lot, he removed the orange cone and motioned me into the space nearest the dancers' entrance. Someone else was parked there now.

As I approached the first car, a large man wearing a dark blue security jacket stepped out of the porn shop adjoining the club. Security: I hadn't thought of that. I wasn't sure he would let me go through with it.

The words *Go in confidence* radiated from within me. Before the security guard could even open his mouth, I briskly approached him and stuck out my hand.

'Hi. My name is Harmony. I used to work here. I just wanted to leave these little notes for the girls.' I whipped out the postcards and presented them to him. He looked at them and back at me. Tilting his head, he seemed caught off guard by the whole thing.

'All right; go ahead,' he said, as he waved me along and went back into the porn shop.

Quickly, before he changed his mind, I placed each postcard on the windshields of the dancers' cars. I wondered what they would think when they found the postcards at the end of the night. What would I have thought?

I imagined myself walking to my car after a long night of work: feet aching, head throbbing from six hours of pounding music. How would I feel if I entered the buzzing silence of my car and saw that little postcard sitting beneath my windshield wiper?

'You are loved... You are welcome here.' Aren't those the words I had always longed to hear? That is all I ever wanted... to be loved and welcomed. Isn't that what we all want?

The whole thing had me thinking, maybe this was the start of something. Maybe I could start going to other clubs throughout the city. I wondered if any other women would want to join me.

I had no idea that within a year a group of volunteers would be going to over 150 strip clubs annually. That we would be walking alongside women, encouraging them to live the healthy, flourishing lives they were created to live. That within two years we would be an official non-profit organization. That four years later we would be training other outreach groups throughout the nation.

The idea I had that night sitting in the parking lot has expanded and become more than I ever dreamed possible. No matter how much it has grown and changed, the message is still the same...

'You are loved. You are welcome here.' In our churches, in our lives.

This very message was first breathed like oxygen into my heart during a time when I needed it most in my own life. My passion to share it was born out of my own broken past. This is my story.

One

SEARCHING

... TO THE HUNGRY, EVEN WHAT IS BITTER TASTES SWEET.

Proverbs 27:7

Thirteen

Derrick sat in the office chair beside my bed and watched me sleep. I never heard him walk into my room that morning. He was sort of stealthy, like that. Long and lanky, with a swift, quiet gait. I didn't know he was there until he yanked the covers off me. I shot up, ready to fight, but relaxed when I realized it was him. He was leaning over the bed, and I could smell the fruity scent of his Let's Jam hair gel. His hair was trimmed into a neat fade. The top was long, combed back into perfect waves.

'What are you doing?' I grumbled, pulling the covers back over my head.

'The side door was open.'

'I know.'

'You know, you really shouldn't leave it open like that.'

He wasn't the first person to say that. My Daddy Russ, the stepfather that raised me, said the same thing when I was eight. It was during the lecture he gave me after a man broke in and nearly beat my mother to death. I saw her after she was discharged from the hospital, and she was ashamed to be seen. Her lips were nearly black and had been stitched back onto her bruised and swollen face. My father dragged me down the long hallway from her bedroom to the side door for a lesson.

25

'You see this? This is how he got in! I don't know why your mother insists on leaving every goddamn door and window in this house open!' my dad hollered. I think he blamed himself for not being home to protect her, that night. Powerlessness and fear can make a person angry.

Five years later, my Daddy Russ had long since moved out. We still left the side door open. And the windows. I know it doesn't make sense, but that's kind of the way my family works. We also left our car doors unlocked – no matter how many times a homeless man slept in it, or the radio got stolen. My mom said that if someone was going to break in, she'd rather not have to replace the radio *and* fix a broken window.

I guess Derrick's family didn't adopt the same philosophy, because he too complained about the side door being left open.

'It's already noon. Why are you still in bed? And where's your mom?' he said, pulling the covers back off me.

'Geeez! Leave me aloooooone! She's in Canada.'

'Canada?' He looked at me, bewildered. 'When did that happen?'

'After Nathaniel left. She went to meet him. She's only supposed to be gone a couple of weeks.' The book of food stamps my mother left me wouldn't last that long, even if I only used them to buy tortillas and butter. I was going to have to start stealing food from the liquor store down the street, pretty soon.

'For real? Are you serious?' His pubescent voice rose and cracked at the end of his sentence.

'I don't care. I like it better with her gone. Plus, MaSyh's coming down to stay with me, so I won't have to take care of Noah by myself.' MaSyh (named after the Maasai Tribe in Africa) was the closest thing to a sister I had. We met when we were two years old and had been inseparable since.

I stood up, stretched, and took in the warm ocean air.

Derrick followed me to the bathroom.

'Harm, seriously. Who is watching you guys?'

'No one. Daddy Russ stops by after work sometimes.'

Derrick stood in the doorway to the bathroom, trying to make sense of it all. Out of habit, he ran his finger along the collar of his crisp white T-shirt to straighten out any creases or wrinkles.

'Come on, get out. I have to pee,' I whined, before nudging him out of the door and pushing it shut.

All Derrick knew was that Nathaniel was the weird boyfriend my mother met at a Narcotics Anonymous meeting. With all the eccentric people we met at those meetings, in some ways life got even more colorful after she got sober.

Nathaniel looked like David Carradine in *Kung Fu* and he walked around our house doing his fancy karate moves like some kind of mysterious, nunchuck-carrying hero. He did fan kicks across my face, barely missing my nose, and randomly placed my brother in headlocks, telling him, 'I could kill you right now if I wanted to.' Derrick didn't like him, because he was pompous and annoying. I didn't like him, because he was worse than those things. Every time he came into my room at night – professing his attraction, rubbing his hands along my body, trying to kiss me – the anger in me festered. I wanted to grab him by the hair and punch him in the mouth. Instead, I lay there, stiff and fearful, begging for him to leave me alone.

That stiffening feeling was familiar to me. Throughout my life, I'd been sexually abused by several people, both men and women. I was exposed to pornography at the age of three by a male relative. 'Stay still. Go to sleep,' I remember him saying. The pink fleshy images on the television screen were burned into my mind.

Staying still and pretending I was asleep was the very

defensive tactic I used the first time it happened. I was five years old, and two women, family friends, said we were going to have a slumber party. The idea seemed fun, until they undressed and told me to take off my pajamas. Hard as I tried, I could not erase the events that followed from my mind. The next morning, we all ate eggs Benedict and drank Sunny Delight as though nothing happened.

The next time, I was about seven. The boy was older than me, and had already threatened to smash my fingers in a vice grip unless I did what he said. So when he told me to take my panties off, I listened. I thought that he would hurt me if I didn't. I believed that there must be something inherently wrong with me that kept attracting those situations. It was as if there was something dirty about me that drew these people and their perversion.

I hated Nathaniel. I hated the way his breath smelled like sour milk, and the way his nostrils made a whistling sound when he breathed. I was relieved he was finally gone. The truth is, I didn't mind my mom being gone, either, even if it meant I had to take care of my eight-year-old brother Noah. I was glad to have the freedom.

When I stepped out of the bathroom, Derrick was still standing in the hallway. His arms were folded across his chest, and he looked around, as though he was assessing his surroundings and getting ready to take charge; like he had been waiting for an opportunity to do so.

'This place is a mess,' he said, peering over my shoulder into the bathroom.

'Yeah. What's new?' I said, kicking a balled-up sock down the hall. The place was always a mess.

'There are a million cats pissing all over your mom's bedroom. The dishes look like they haven't been done for weeks.

And this bathroom is disgusting! It's just nasty.' He made a face, like he just smelled a waft of something horrible.

'It's not my fault that two of the cats had kittens at the same time. They're too little to use the litter box.' There were 17 of them, in total.

He paused, and looked at me like I was going to have to come up with a better excuse than that.

'What do you want me to do about it? The house is always like this,' I reasoned.

He stepped into the tiny bathroom where the sink, toilet and tub were all crammed against each other. A person could stand up from using the toilet and bend over to wash their hands without having to take a step. Derrick peered into the toilet bowl, which was covered with a pinkish orange film. There were old cotton balls, hairballs, and crumpled toilet paper on the white tile floor. Mildew and rust lined the toilet, bathtub and sink.

Derrick's face was all scrunched and twisted, as if he had been holding his breath in a sewage tank. His big brown eyes pinched together at the corners and he took a swift step back, out of the bathroom.

'You know you have to clean it. You can't live like this.'

'It's my house. I can live how I want to.' I enjoyed being able to say this to someone.

'Do you really *want* to live like this?'

I looked at the bathroom and considered his question. It really was pretty gross.

I thought of Pippi Longstocking. How she got to live by herself with a monkey and tied scrub brushes to her feet to wash the floor. Slipping and sliding in the suds looked like so much fun. I always wanted to be like her and live on my own. Carefree and independent. But I don't think her floors had furry, toxic growth like my bathroom did.

Derrick wasn't going to let up. And I didn't much enjoy the dirt, either. That's why I spent most of my time locked away in the converted service porch I slept in. There was hardly enough room for my twin mattress, but at least the place was clean.

'Fine. We can clean,' I submitted.

'We. There's no we in this. This isn't my house.' Derrick walked away, leaving me to my duties.

I poked my head into the bedroom where Noah was still sleeping to enlist his help.

'Noah, it's time to wake up. We have to clean up this house,' I barked. I gave the orders, but I knew it would be at least half an hour before he would finally roll out of bed. He was a hard sleeper and woke up about as fast as a sloth runs a marathon.

Then I stomped off into the kitchen, where I had to destroy a spider's web to get to the cleanser under the sink. I dumped Comet all over the sink and tub; after about 20 minutes of pushing a sponge around, I grew tired of cleaning and joined Derrick in the living room, where he was watching television.

'Are you finished?'

'Yeah.' I certainly *wanted* to be finished.

'Let's see.'

I followed him back to the bathroom to inspect my work. Before he even stepped inside, he whipped around and looked at me as if I had lost my mind.

'Seriously? You're done? You think this is clean? You're going to have to do better than that.'

He went to the kitchen and brought back gloves, a bucket and some bleach.

'Here, fill this up with hot water and let's put some bleach in there. Hasn't anyone ever taught you how to clean a bathroom?'

The truth is, nobody had. He sat in the doorway and guided

me through the process. After an hour of scrubbing and rinsing and scrubbing and rinsing, the tiles were more white than green and the toilet actually looked as if you could sit on it without contracting a virus. I was proud of my work. And I wasn't bothered that Derrick didn't help me. I was thankful that he cared. He cared about whether or not my bathroom was clean and he cared enough to take the time to show me how to clean it.

The truth is, I never liked having a dirty bathroom. Like everything else in my life that was dirty or embarrassing, I learned to live with it. And, when necessary, I pretended it wasn't there. When friends came to visit, I never pointed out the dirt and apologized, as some people would. I just held my breath and hoped that somehow – some way – they wouldn't notice. Derrick was the first person to point out the dirt. And he showed me how to get rid of it. I felt thankful; indebted, even.

Fifteen

The light from the street lamps on Pico Boulevard dissipated into the thick ocean air, creating an orange fog. My mother's van came to a stop near the liquor store, and I held the stare of a homeless man gripping the crumpled paper bag containing his drink. The whites of his eyes shone like yellow moons against his midnight skin.

'We're right by Derrick's house.' My head whipped around to see where my mother was pointing.

'We are?' Though we had driven down this street on countless occasions, everything seemed new in light of this information.

'How do you know?' I turned and looked at my mother skeptically. In the three years I had known him, Derrick had been so secretive about where he lived. Why would he tell her where he lived and not me?

'I took him home the other night, when he missed the ten o'clock bus.'

Funny that she hadn't mentioned it until now.

'Really, I would have thought he'd have you drop him off down the street, or something. You actually saw his house?'

'There's a lot about him that you don't know.' She turned to look at me; her almond-shaped eyes were cloudy emeralds.

'Like what?' I prodded.

'Well, sweetie, he told me in confidence. Let's just say he has some serious issues with his adoptive mother.'

'Adopted? He was adopted?'

She rolled down her window; the cold, dense air coursed through the van and gave me a shiver. Plucking and lighting a cigarette from the pack of American Spirits in her console, she left me in suspense. Her cheeks hollowed methodically with each drag, accentuating her round, Cherokee bone structure. Her Native American features were contrasted by long, flowing, strawberry-blonde hair and sun-sensitive German skin.

'Mom… Derrick was adopted?' I prodded.

'Honey, I thought he told you that.' Her sympathetic look was meant for both Derrick and me: him for his apparently troubled life, and me for not knowing about it.

'No. He never mentioned that. What else did he tell you?'

'Like I said, he told me in confidence. I just wanted you to be aware.'

There was tenderness in her voice. I could tell that her attitude towards him had changed. Until this point, he had just been another kid that showed up on her doorstep to hang out with her daughter. Now he was so much more. He was a potential rescue.

As a skinny little string-bean of a kid, with bright red hair and freckles, my mother would have had a difficult time making friends even if she hadn't moved around so much. Her father was a jazz drummer for a military band, so she and her parents jumped from base to base. Being an only child, with no siblings to offer her camaraderie, made her even more isolated.

While all her 'army brat' friends woke up early on Sunday mornings to wear frilly little church dresses, her beatnik parents recovered from long nights in the jazz clubs. Being one of the few non-Christian children on base solidified her status as an outsider; most of the other parents wouldn't even let their children play with her, since her family didn't think and act like theirs.

When she was a teen, her family picked up and moved to Vegas, where my grandfather was the drummer for the house band at the Stardust. While he played with all of the greats, from Frank Sinatra to Dean Martin, my mother ran the streets with a crowd of rebels and revolutionaries. Rather than trying to conform to the standards of all the squares, she relished her outsider status and aligned herself with outcasts and underdogs.

And it wasn't only people. Animals would do. In many cases they were preferable to people, because they weren't likely to ditch their caretaker. From a crow with a broken wing to a freshwater turtle abandoned at the beach with red graffiti on its shell, my mother had a gift for restoring hope and health in the lost and broken. If anyone could rescue Derrick, she could. Maybe we both could.

Finding no comfort in the large black stone my mother placed on my stomach, I rolled onto my side, tightened up into a ball and let out a whimper. My mother walked back into the living room, where I was lying in her bed.

'Is the stone working?' she asked, in her soothing, caretaker voice.

'No. Nothing is working,' I whined.

'Here, take this,' she offered, with a wise and knowing look on her face.

'What is it?'

'Gin Bo. It's illegal here in the States, but I know a man from China who has access to it. It will help your cramps. It will also help you sleep.'

I opened my palm to receive the tiny white pill. A pill that small hardly looked as though it would do anything to take the edge off of the extraordinary pain I was in. I placed the pill on my tongue and took it with my mother's tea, made from fresh peppermint and chamomile. As I sipped the steaming concoction, another wave of pain swept through my abdomen with a force that could propel a ten-pound child from my loins. I imagined that the contractions mimicked the pain a woman feels during childbirth. *No other 15-year-old has cramps like this! It's not fair!* I screamed inside.

I sat up and tried rocking back and forth to distract myself from the pain. After a few minutes, the cramping dulled, and I began to feel the muscles in my arms and legs become heavy and relaxed. My head became light and floaty. The Gin Bo was working. I leaned back against my mother's soft, worn pillows and took in the faint smell of mugwort. Then I heard a knock at the door. My mother got up to answer it, and I assumed that it was one of her friends coming over for a late-night cigarette and venting session. They always knew they could come to our house to talk about their woes.

It took me a moment to register Derrick's face, which was half covered by a black baseball cap pulled low on his forehead. The hood from his black sweatshirt was pulled over his head and covered the sides of his face. He looked as if he was hiding from someone. I wondered if he was worried about walking across the Venice border at night. In summers past, he had always made sure to be on his bus back to Santa Monica by sunset.

'Hey, Derrick, what's going on?' my mother said as she took him into her arms. He did not return her embrace, but neither did he seem to mind it.

'Come on in,' my mother said nurturingly.

'Hey, Harm,' he said, acknowledging my presence in a deep, monotone voice. 'Diana, can we talk?' he continued.

'Sure. Come on back to the kitchen. Would you like some tea?' She smiled. Her cheeks were like red apples, nestling beneath her almond eyes.

I wondered if Derrick's mother had had another of her episodes and kicked him out of the house in a fit of unfounded fury. It was probably about the chair. It was always about that chair. From what Derrick told me, his mother had a big upholstered chair in her house, and her rage centered on that darn chair like planets around the sun. She would come into his room at night to state her case.

'Somebody done gone and ruined my chair. You wanna tell me who did this?' Groggily, he would follow her to the chair, where she would yell, 'Look at it! Look at what you've done to my chair!'

'Mom, there's nothing there. Nobody ruined your chair.'

'Get out! Get out of my house!' she would demand. And that's how the story went.

Fighting drowsiness, I strained to hear what Derrick and my mother were talking about in the next room. Their voices were low whispers, and I couldn't make out what they were saying. After a few minutes, my mother came back into the living room and sat at the edge of her bed.

'Harmony, how do you feel about Derrick staying here for a while?'

I lifted my heavy eyelids as wide as I could and answered, 'Yeah, that's fine.' As I drifted off to sleep, I wondered if it was the chair.

One night, a few weeks after Derrick moved in, we were both home and bored. Including Derrick, there were no less than nine people living in our two-bedroomed home, but things were surprisingly quiet that night. Michelle was on 3rd Street Promenade with her boyfriend Fonzie, doing psychic readings for tourists and other marks. Joe was probably out selling his laced weed. I never knew where Layla was floating about. She didn't have a job, but she left every morning, brisk and early, and at the end of the day, she tiptoed into the living room and set up a massage table, where she would sleep for the night. She wasn't home yet, either. My brother Noah was in the front room playing Sonic the Hedgehog with Hawk, the displaced Native American boy my mom took in as a favor to a friend. And my mother was spending the night at her boyfriend's house. That left Derrick and me alone in the bedroom we normally shared with Noah, Hawk, and Joe.

I lay across the futon and pulled at the feather of a handmade dream catcher nailed to the wall. Derrick twisted rhythmically from side to side in an office chair while meticulously shaping the bill of his navy blue baseball cap. It had to be curved into a perfect C.

Derrick came up with a solution to our boredom. 'Wanna play poker?'

'I don't know how to play.'

'Come on, I'll teach you.'

If it was going to be anything like our domino matches, I

was sure to lose. He was a much better player than me, but even when I *could* win, I didn't. This went against the grain of my highly competitive nature, but when Derrick lost, nobody was happy. If the game wasn't going his way, he would get mad and sulk around, or strike his hand across the domino formation to ruin the game before his fate as a loser could be solidified.

At first, I protested. 'I was going to win that round!'

'No you weren't! You really think you can beat me? Derricks don't get beat,' he argued assuredly.

Tired of his tantrums, I finally gave up trying to win, and if by sheer luck I got an unbeatable hand, I still let him win.

We played a practice round of poker, and he carefully explained what hand beat what. I did my best to follow, but it was too much to keep track of. In true Derrick fashion, one hand was all the grace I got. From that point on, it was up to me to play the hand I was dealt, no guidance given, no questions asked. And of course, one hand after another, I lost. Again and again.

At first, his eyes lit up and he took pleasure in beating me. He threw his head back and laughed each time. 'Rack 'em up!' he said, pointing to the cards, so that I would shuffle the deck after each hand.

After five or six hands, winning must have lost its ego-stroking power. He sighed heavily.

'This game sucks.'

'What do you want to do?'

'I have an idea.' His eyes flickered with mischief. 'Let's play strip poker…'

'Nooooooo…' I said, laughing nervously at the thought of his suggestion.

'Why not?'

'Cause I'm gonna lose, that's why…'

'Come on. I'll be nice. Siiiiike!'

'No way. I'm not playing that with you.'

'Seriously, let's play. It'll be fun.'

'Fine. Only if I can put on extra clothes.' I figured it would make the night more interesting.

'OK,' he said, as though it would hardly keep me from losing. And he was right.

One by one, I peeled off layers of sweatshirts, T-shirts, hats, and sweatpants, until I stood before him blushing red and stripped down to my bra and panties.

'You have a nice body,' he said, evaluating me.

'OK, that's enough. I'm putting my clothes back on.'

'No. That's not the deal. You still have to take your panties off. I won that round.'

'Fine,' I said, standing and pulling them up and down in a flash. I got dressed and we sat across from each other in silence.

'I'm bored,' he finally offered.

My eyes met his. *I just took off all of my clothes for him and he has the nerve to say that he's bored!* I thought. He read my expression and realized my distaste at his comment.

'No, I mean. That was cool and all. But let's up the ante.'

'What do you mean?'

'Let's play for something else.'

'Like money?'

'No, not money… something better.'

'Like what?'

'Like…'

'Like what?' I prompted.

'Sex,' he said quickly, as if to take away the meaning of the word.

'What??' He had to be kidding.

'If you lose, we have sex. If you win, we don't.'

I was pretty sure he was bluffing. Not positive, but pretty

sure. I didn't want to have sex with him. I was bored too, but not that bored. Would he really expect me to pay up? I said yes. I had nothing to gain and everything to lose, but I still said yes.

I knew I was set to lose the hand as he dealt it. The air was thick with suspense. As if I had a shot at victory, I played my best. I lost. He wasn't bluffing.

We had sex. I wagered my body in a game of cards and we had sex. I can remember being thankful that he didn't rape me. 'Are you sure this is OK?' he asked, and I was taken by the very thought that I had a choice in the matter. I had a choice. It was mine and I could choose. Still, my body did what it had been trained to do. It was still and heavy, naked and yielding. I chose the only thing I knew how to choose: surrender.

Casual sex. Is that what grown-ups have? No ties. No attachments. Sex for the sake of sex. I wanted to be a grown-up about it; to act like one of those mature, independent women with a corporate job. The one who gets out of bed first after a one-night stand, slips on her pumps and skirt suit and leaves the man lying alone in a their hotel room, wanting her more for leaving him. I wanted to be that woman, but I couldn't. There was nothing casual or meaningless about it for me. I had given a piece of myself to him and the only way to keep from losing part of me was to keep him near.

The next morning, I lay in bed listening to the shower run on the other side of the bedroom wall. Was he leaving? For the day? For good? The mere idea of this punched me with fear. He tiptoed into the bedroom wearing his dark blue jeans and a crisp white T-shirt. His long wavy brown hair was pulled into a neat ponytail. He was definitely leaving.

'Hey, where are you going?' I had to know.

Derrick looked up at me, tilting his head with a grin. He seemed amused that I cared.

'Why do you want to know?' The power shift in our relationship was tangible. Until this point, it was he who wondered about me. It was he who subtly wedged his way into my world.

'Just wondering. You know… I don't know. I just thought we could hang out today.' The words stumbled out of my mouth.

'Naw, man. I gotta go.'

The thought of him leaving me made me feel vulnerable and inadequate. Hadn't I already given him enough to make him want to stay? I never should have slept with him, I thought.

'Where are you going?' As the words were coming out of my mouth I knew I shouldn't have asked again. I should have played it cool, as if I didn't care. I should have acted nonchalant about the whole thing to get my power back; but the fear of loss had its grip on me.

'Out. I'm going out.' He laughed as he said it. My desperation seemed to flatter him.

'A'ight then. Peace,' he said, as he walked away, leaving me wanting him more for it.

Sixteen

Maybe it was because he wouldn't get a job. Or maybe it was because my mother realized, years before I ever did, that Derrick would not be rescued. After several months of quiet discussions behind closed doors, and numerous inquiries as to what jobs he had applied for, my mother put her foot down, and Derrick was packing his bags.

'Where will you go? What are you going to do?' I pleaded through salty tears.

'I'll figure something out. Don't worry about me.' His response did nothing to ease my anxiety.

'You can't just be out there on the streets. What are you going to do? And when will I see you?'

I opened my sock drawer and reached in the back, where I had a small stash of money hidden. I had saved it from my summer job selling T-shirts on the Boardwalk for Greenpeace. I pulled out a small stack of $20 bills and handed it to him.

'Here. Just in case you need it,' I offered.

'I'll be around,' he said, as he took the money from my hands. And with that, he was gone.

I stayed awake at night, wondering where he was. I worried that he was sleeping on the streets somewhere, but I knew he was more resourceful that that. While picturing him homeless struck pity in my heart, it was the alternative that I most feared.

What if someone else was taking care of him? What if he didn't need me any more? As long as he was living in my household, I had something to offer him; some incentive for him to stick around. All of that was gone now. I had nothing to give him. What if he was driven into the arms of another by sheer necessity?

A few days later, he called and asked me to meet him at the Santa Monica Mall. I rushed there as fast as I could. When I arrived, he was sitting at the bus stop with his head down and his elbows propped up on his legs. He looked up at me as I stepped off the bus. I wore my hair slicked back tightly into a bun, just as he liked it, my favorite overalls, and a white T-shirt cropped just below the bra. I wanted to remind him of what he had left behind. I watched him take in the sight of my bare waist. My plan was working.

'Hey, Der,' I greeted him.

'What's up?' He was never one for hugging, but I had hoped

that our reunion would warrant it. It didn't.

'How are you? How have you been?' I asked.

'A'ight, I guess.'

'I've missed you.' I said it knowing that he wouldn't reciprocate, but I didn't take it personally. He needed to act hard to protect his soft, wounded heart. In time, I could show him that he could trust me.

'Is that right?' he said, smiling. 'I wanted to see you so I could say goodbye,' he continued.

'Goodbye? What do you mean, goodbye? Where are you going?'

'Away.'

'Away where? For how long?'

'For a while. Probably a long time.'

I couldn't hold back the tears that were welling up in my eyes.

'I'm thinking of joining the army.' He looked off into the distance as he said it.

'What!? The army? Are you kidding me?' His leaving was bad enough, but the army! He could get killed.

'I don't see any other options.'

'No. I am sorry, but you are not going to the army,' I said firmly.

'Then what am I supposed to do? You tell me.' This time he looked directly at me. The intensity in his eyes struck me silent. 'That's what I thought. Nothing. There's nothing else I can do.' His words were sharp and cutting.

I remembered the last time he got caught up in something potentially life-threatening. He never told me the details. All he said was, he needed money right away or something terrible would happen. He couldn't tell me. He didn't want to get me involved in it. How was he supposed to get the money? I came up with a solution and we walked to the ATM machine, where I pulled out $300 from my savings account. It was the money I had been saving for a car. But Derrick needed it. He needed me. And here we were again. I knew what he wanted from me. And if I didn't come up with a way to save him from going to the army, some other girl would.

'You can get an apartment. We can find you one for really cheap down in Venice.'

'And just how am I supposed to pay rent at this apartment?' His voice was almost taunting.

'I'll help you. I'll get a job. We can do this, we can make this happen. I just don't want you going off and getting yourself killed in the army. I couldn't live with myself.'

And so it was settled. He would get an apartment and I would get a job. The arrangement worked for both of us. It kept him alive and it prevented him from leaving me.

Seventeen

Just after my seventeenth birthday I was hired at a coffee shop in Santa Monica. Derrick was safe and sound, living in a single apartment in Venice. I, on the other hand, was not doing so well. One morning, I had a huge blow-out with my mother, after she read my journal and discovered I had been sleeping with Derrick. 'I took that boy into my home and all the while you were in here shacking up with him!' she screamed.

I could see the fury in her eyes. The fight was escalating rapidly, and I decided to stop it the only way I knew how – by running. I grabbed my overnight bag, which was always packed in case I had to get out fast, and started for the door. When she first grabbed me, I am sure she only meant to restrain me from leaving, but her temper got the better of her. It wasn't until her boyfriend came running in and pulled her off me that I was finally able to make my escape.

I sat on the bus bench in Santa Monica, hugging the tattered koala bear I took everywhere with me. Even at 17, I couldn't sleep without him. I wasn't sure where to go. I was familiar with only two major bus routes: one that would take me to Venice; the other to Hollywood. I had no reason to go to either place. I had no reason to stay where I was. I had no reasons, no plan. I had nothing but my teddy bear and the backpack I kept beside my bed, packed and ready, just in case I ran away or my mom kicked me out… again.

A champagne-colored Lexus pulled in front of the bus stop. The driver was a middle-aged woman who looked as if she smelled of gardenias and hairspray. Her large diamond ring caught the light and cast rainbows on the dashboard of her car. In the passenger seat was a young girl – her daughter perhaps – with silky golden hair cascading down her shoulders. The young girl said something and her mother tossed her head back in a laugh. Their connection was palpable, and I longed for what they had.

As they drove away, I imagined that they were headed down to their house in Malibu, tucked against a canyon, overlooking the Pacific Ocean: a place where clean, white refrigerators were always stocked with brand-named food. The daughter would go to her perfect pink bedroom and sprawl out on her bed to do homework. At 6.30 pm the mother would call her family to the dinner table, where they would tell each other about their day. I wanted to be that girl. I wanted a home that *felt* like home.

I called my biological father from a payphone outside the Santa Monica mall to tell him about the blow-out with my mom. Even *he* wouldn't want his own daughter wandering the streets at night. What would people at his fancy corporate job think? As I thought about it, I wondered if they even knew he had a daughter. I called him, and his secretary patched me through.

'This is Bill.' He was sharp and professional.

'Dad, it's Harmony.' His tone didn't change when he realized it was me. He had planes to catch and meetings to attend. I was a relic from his past: a dusty souvenir on the top shelf of his closet, reminding him of a brief time when he grew his hair long and walked barefoot around the campus of University of California at Los Angeles pretending he wasn't a capitalist Republican.

Unabashedly, I stated my case and asked him for help. His response was clear. He didn't need a new room-mate, and he wasn't interested in making a charitable contribution to my cause. In the end, I couldn't close the deal and he had to get back to work.

I squeezed my teddy bear to my chest and rested my cheek on top of his scratchy head. I pictured my father cuddled up at night in his king-size bed with fluffy pillows. Of course, I had hoped he would offer me a plane ticket to Chicago to stay with him. He had enough spare bedrooms to accommodate me in that giant home overlooking acres of suburban trees. But I would have settled for a motel room for the night. As I contemplated this, I told myself that it was his newest wife that didn't want me there. That was easier to accept than the alternative.

The summer sky was fading into a deeper shade of blue, and I knew the sun would be going down in an hour or so. I didn't know where to go, but my instinct told me to keep moving. So I got on the next bus back to Venice and headed towards the beach. It was the most familiar to me.

I stood at the edge of the bike path, overlooking the small rolling mounds of sand that stretched out to the ocean. The wind whipped my sandy-blonde hair into and out of my face. A camp of seagulls fought over an abandoned bag of French fries. One whisked it into the air, before dropping it. Three others pulled at the paper until it tore apart and French fries were flung all over the sand. This caused a frenzy among the other seagulls. Dozens of seagulls yakked and gulled as they dove in for their share of the booty.

What do I do now? This question pressed itself against the inside of my lips, so that I wanted to shout it out for someone to hear. That is when I remembered the number Derrick had given me.

'If you can't find a place tonight, call this hotline and tell them what happened. They will tell you what to do.'

Of course, I couldn't stay with him any longer; not with my mother threatening to have him arrested for aiding and abetting a minor. It was just as well for him. Having me stay in his apartment – the apartment I paid for, mind you – put a cramp in his game. I used the sleeve of my shirt to wipe off the payphone and made the call. After I had recounted all the details of the fight with my mother, the woman at the hotline asked me a question.

'Would you feel safe to return home?' Her voice was warm and caring.

I paused and thought carefully about what it meant to feel safe. I knew I wouldn't die if I returned home. Until that incident, my mother had never left bruises before. But was it safe? Was it ever safe? *What is safe?* I wasn't completely sure. The home that I pictured the mother and daughter in the Lexus going to was what I imagined 'safe' to be. Whether or not my mother's house was safe, one thing was certain: I didn't want to go back.

'No. I wouldn't feel safe going back to that house,' I replied.

I followed her directions to a group home. It was a quaint

little house, sitting behind lavish green landscape in a middle-class neighborhood near Santa Monica College. As I approached the house, I wondered if a neighbor would have mistaken me for a teenager returning home from an afternoon at the movies with her friends. I wrapped one arm tightly around my teddy bear and felt my heart pounding as I knocked on the front door.

A middle-aged man wearing a jogging suit let me in to the dim front room, where a stalky teenaged boy was sprawled on an old couch watching Yo MTV raps. He lifted his head in a nod to acknowledge my presence as I walked by.

'Come on back and I'll show you your room, so you can get settled. We only have one other girl tonight, so you have your own room for now. The boys sleep at the other end of the hall. You'll do your intake tomorrow, so you can just relax tonight.'

Knowing that there were boys in the same home was unsettling. I wondered if there would be someone awake in the middle of the night to stop them from sneaking into my room.

The bedroom he showed me into had two bunk beds in it. I headed straight for the bottom bunk, furthest from the door, and noticed the window next to it. As I peeked through the curtain, I felt relieved when I saw the iron bars. The boys down the hall wouldn't be able to climb out of their window and sneak in through mine. I would just have to keep my eye on the door and listen for footsteps in the hall.

The next day I had my intake meeting. A handsome man in his twenties named Jermaine called me into the tiny office in the front of the house. He was wearing a dark blue windbreaker jumpsuit like the ones basketball players wear. He was the kind of guy that my friends and I would have stopped to gawk at if we had seen him in the mall. 'He's fine,' we would whisper as he passed by. Before he got into the real questions, he warmed me up with small talk.

'What school do you go to?'

'I was at Fairfax, but I am supposed to go to Santa Monica High when the summer's over.'

'I went to Samo too.' Common ground. I was beginning to feel more at ease.

'Oh, really? When did you graduate?'

'I graduated in '90. Took some time off, but now I am at Santa Monica College.'

I wondered whether I knew a lot of the same people.

'What do you study?'

'Poli-sci. One day, I'm going to be the first black President of the United States.' He shifted in his chair and cleared his throat. I stared at him, waiting for him to laugh and say he was joking. Who actually believes they can be President?

It wasn't a joke. I supposed he could be the President. Someone has to be President. Why not him? The audacity of this hope made me want to hope for something too.

The interview continued. Questions, questions and more questions: Full name? Age? Date of birth? Place of birth? Mother's name? Address? Siblings? Have you ever been raped? *Have you ever been raped?*

I sat and stared out of the bay window at the quiet street outside. Silence. No one had ever asked me that question. It caught me off guard. He asked casually, calmly, like it happens all the time. I answered casually, calmly, like it happens all the time: 'Yes.'

He explained his status as a mandated reporter, and that if I told him the name of the person he would have to report it.

'Would he get arrested?' I asked.

'Maybe.'

The memory of the first rape jolted through my mind.

48

My ex-boyfriend Maurice and I had left the party we were at to meander about a residential neighborhood, passing amber-lit windows and French doors revealing Jewish families dining together in honor of Shabbat. I began to feel hopeful. *Maybe we would get back together. Maybe we could be a family, some day.*

Behind the walls of a cobblestone, ivy-laced home, a man with a thick black beard bowed his head and prayed, beckoning the rest of his family to join him. There was a girl in a green velvet dress sitting to the left of him. She was probably 14, like me. Her skin was a clean, olive porcelain and her hair was pulled back in a tousled ponytail, with wisps of hair framing her petite face. I wondered if she ever went to parties and had crushes on boys.

Walking next to Maurice, hearing the sound of his feet against crisp leaves and his breath escaping into the cool night air, I felt as though I were standing on the brink of something promising. I imagined Maurice pulling me into his arms and telling me that he never should have let me go. That he couldn't imagine life without me – that every time he heard our song, 'Always and Forever' by Heatwave, it was me he hoped to be with for ever and always. It had been three years since that night.

'Let's say I reported something, but it was a long time ago. Could he still be arrested?' I asked Jermaine.

'As long as it was within the past seven years...' Jermaine let silence rest in the room as I contemplated saying something.

I remembered when we approached that Elementary school. Maurice had been silent for most of the walk. He took me by the hand and quickened his pace.

'Come on,' he said, in a hushed and hurried voice.

When we reached the ten-foot chain-link fence, Maurice let go of my hand, climbed to the top and hoisted himself to the other side.

'Come on,' he repeated, as I nervously surveyed our surroundings.

He stood there with a look of anticipation in his eyes; his body was crouched and his knees slightly bent, as if he would be less visible that way. I didn't want to let him down. I wanted to show him how adventurous I was, so I shakily made my way up and over, the fence wiggling and shuddering beneath me the whole way. The excitement of it all reminded me of the times that my mother would wake my brother Noah and me in the middle of the night, drive us down the coast to the Santa Monica Mountains, and take us on a hike with nothing but the light of the moon to illuminate our path.

As soon as I was over the fence, Maurice darted for the shadows of a stairwell across the barren schoolyard. I chased after him and followed him up the flight of concrete stairs, ducking all the way. When we reached the last stair, Maurice stretched out his neck as he assessed our surroundings and finally breathed a sigh of relief. I sat on the top step and my pulse raced with adrenaline.

'Hi,' he said, grinning and looking at me as if for the first time. His darling array of curls were perched and neatly separated atop his head.

'Hi,' I responded, my lips spreading into a flirtatious smile.

He lifted my chin and gently placed his mouth against mine. My heart fluttered so rapidly I was sure he could hear it beating inside of my chest. Part of me wanted to be the kind of girl that wouldn't make out with a guy who wasn't my boyfriend; but the part of me that wanted to be swept up by unhindered love and show Maurice what he was missing since he broke up with me prevailed.

Maurice's kisses gradually became more rushed and

sloppy. I pulled away and looked at him questioningly. His face snapped back towards me and I stopped his momentum by placing my hand firmly on his chest and resisting. He took both of my shoulders into his hands and pushed me onto the ground by the force of his weight. The sharp cold of the concrete seeped through my shirt and my back jerked into an arch.

'Stop!' I insisted.

'Shhhhh!!!' he hushed me demandingly.

His eyes were wild and focused, looking towards me but at some place beyond me. He leaned forward and his T-shirt fell over my face. Covering my eyes – covering me. He released one of my shoulders and shifted his hand towards the center of my chest, still pressing down on me with the force of his 180-pound frame. Without prevailing, I bat at his hand to try to stop him. When he yanked at my jeans, propelling my hips forward, the small of my back came down hard on the metal ridge that lined the top stair.

Beneath the musk of his shirt, I tried to hold in my tears. Crying would recognize the wrong of it, and the wrong of it was more than I could digest. In the end, I failed. Tears streamed down the side of my temples and onto the concrete beneath me. A familiar, cooling paralysis came over my body, flowing from my neck, through my arms and down the center of my body to my feet. There was a sensation of white noise in my blood and I knew it well. It was the same feeling that had carried me through these sorts of encounters in their various forms in the past. This feeling let me feel absent from situations in which I was forced to be present.

He stood up and rustled into his jeans without acknowledging me. I didn't move at first. I *couldn't* move at first. I crumpled into a ball and sobbed into my knees. He finally looked in my direction.

'Why are you crying?' His eyes pinched at the sides as he asked the question.

The mere mention of crying unleashed a new bout.

'What the hell is wrong with you?' he asked, shaking his head as he turned and started back down the steps.

'Don't leave me here...' I begged, uselessly.

I watched him walk across the yard, only this time he was not ducking or hiding. I sat crouched in a dark stairwell, while he walked confidently, with his head held high, back to the party. I went back and forth between blaming myself and blaming him. Maybe he didn't realize that I didn't want to have sex with him? Maybe it was my fault for going on a walk with him in the first place? I should have known better. He wouldn't have had to force me if I hadn't resisted. But what kind of a jerk has sex with a girl and leaves her alone and crying? Now he is going to think I am dramatic, and he won't want to be with me. In the end, it was easier to blame myself than to make sense of the ambiguity of it all. If it was my fault, I still had control. If blame rested on me, there was always the hope that *I* could change.

It was only after my feet hit the ground on the other side of the fence that I realized I didn't know my way back to the party. We had taken a couple of turns, and I had been too caught up with Maurice to pay attention to where we were going. I headed in the general direction we had come from and wandered up and down streets filled with trees so large they spanned the road and appeared to greet each other at the mid-line. The neighborhood seemed safe enough, complete with working street lamps and chirping crickets; still, my heart pounded with anxiety at the thought of being so lost. So very, very lost.

After winding my way around for an hour, I finally noticed a familiar sight, as the cobblestone house came into view. Dinner was over and the dining room was empty – void of family and prayers. Only the dirty dishes remained, left behind by the satisfied diners.

When I finally heard the music and chatter of the party-goers, from about a half a block away, I did my best to tug through my disheveled hair and wipe the streaking mascara from my cheeks. I hoped to find Maurice sitting in the corner of the room, stewing in remorse and worry over what had happened. Instead, he was standing in the center of the room, telling some stupid joke that sent everyone around him into hysterics. He was perfectly content, his appetite satiated. I was left feeling empty and ashamed – dirty and used. He acted as though nothing had happened. His nonchalance made me question my own sanity. Over the course of the next year, he raped me several more times, each time adding to the shame and disgust I felt. I finally stopped fighting him. If I let him have what he wanted, he couldn't rape me.

'Do you have something you want to tell me?' Jermaine probed gently. His voice broke my trance and brought me back into the small office at the group home.

'Yes. I have been raped…' The words came out of someone else's mouth – someone stronger and more confident than me – '…but I don't know if I want to tell you his name.'

I let it all marinate. Maurice in jail. An image flashed in my head of me on a witness stand, recalling the rapes; being questioned; blamed. People forming opinions; pointing fingers; whispering names.

'No. I don't want to tell you his name,' I resolved.

I walked by the phone at the group home every few minutes, each time hoping that Tisha, another resident, had finally finished her conversation with whomever it was she was talking to. She was slumped over on a stool, and her plump brown cheek was pressed against the receiver as she whispered and giggled intermittently. If I didn't call Derrick right then, I wouldn't have another chance until the next day during phone hours.

'Tisha, I still need to use the phone…' I finally interrupted.

She smacked her teeth and looked up at me, annoyed.

'Please. I really need to use it.'

She took a deep breath, before ending her conversation. 'I've gotta go. That white girl I was telling you about has to use the phone.'

'Thanks, Tisha,' I said as she hung up.

'That's all right. It was just that guy I met at the mall with Kayla yesterday.'

The other girls in the home went to the mall without me, and most everywhere else, for that matter. While they were enjoying a summer of free day passes for good behavior to do fun things, such as going to the beach, I was using my passes to work. Sometimes they would stop by the coffee shop where I worked to say 'Hi!' and to tell me about all the phone numbers they had got that day.

'You should have seen this freak I was talking to! He looked good!' they'd brag about the day's conquests. Standing there with fudge smudges on my white apron, smelling as if I took baths in coffee beans, I listened longingly to all the fun they were having.

I sat on the chair, which was still warm from Tisha sitting there for so long, and made the call. Finally, an answer.

'Hey Der!' I couldn't contain my thrill at hearing his voice.

'Oh, hi. What's up?'

'I've been trying to call you, but there's never any answer. Where've you been?'

Silence. He didn't like being questioned.

'Well, I'm leaving here soon,' I said.

'Already?' Already? It had been almost a month! And he hadn't even been to see me during visiting hours.

'Don't sound so disappointed.'

'I'm not. I mean the time just kind of flew by.' He tried to recover.

'There aren't any foster homes available in the area, and I don't want to go all the way out to Lancaster. The social worker said I can't emancipate, 'cuz the court process would take too long and I'm almost 18 anyway. So I'm going back home.'

'Are you sure that's a good idea?'

'School's going to be starting back up. Plus I am going to keep working, so it's not like I will have to be home that much…'

Most importantly, I would be back in Venice, close to him. Besides, I knew I wouldn't have to be back at home much longer. After the school year was over, I would be turning 18 and could get my own place.

Eighteen

I pushed the front door open gently and tiptoed into the apartment, which smelled like fresh paint. Running my hand along the wall, I found a light switch. 'Dang, no electricity,' I whispered to myself. Once my eyes adjusted to the darkness, I crept over to the kitchen counter to set my purse down.

You don't have to sneak around, I told myself. This is your apartment. This is home. I had already paid my first month's rent and security deposit, but the idea of having my own place was still new.

My mother's words rang in my head: 'You'll be back.'

I'll be back? Why on earth would I go back? Picking up extra shifts at my job at the coffee shop, saving every dime I could, planning, budgeting, and finally convincing the manager of this building to allow me to sign the lease before my eighteenth birthday. No, I would never go back.

This is my home, I thought to myself as I stood in the center of the dark, empty living room. I kicked my sandals off and let my feet sink into the carpet – my carpet. Walking through the apartment, I peeked inside closets and cabinets, imagining how they would look with my clothes and belongings in them. I realized I would have to stop by a local store and buy a bath towel.

The bedroom was spacious, much bigger than the one I was used to. Drawing the bedroom curtains, I looked out onto the quiet West Los Angeles street below and watched a jogger with a golden retriever round the bend. Although it was only a ten-minute drive from Venice, it felt like a different world altogether.

I would miss Venice. For nearly 18 years, it was the unchanging ground beneath my feet. Dreadlocked Rastafarians drumming on bongos with thick, rough hands and sun-weathered skin. Gang bangers lined up near Windward Avenue, wearing dark blue dickeys and blue rags – standing cool and hard, watching 16-year-old girls in jeans and gold nugget earrings walk by, pushing strollers. Circles of tranced hippies on laced weed, dancing and dancing to set the sun orange and purple.

My mother was a part of Venice, too: selling crystals and hand-made jewelry to make a dollar; holding her ground with wild, strawberry, wind-blown hair and contemplating, green eyes. I can picture myself, a barefoot hippy child with beach-blonde hair and tanned skin covered in white, salty residue. Running through hot sands, I would throw myself into the polluted grey waters, splashing and diving until I was breathless and delirious.

Yes, I would miss living in Venice, where a urine-stained homeless man would tell your mama if he saw you stealing from the liquor store. Eyes always watching and knowing, without conversation or formalities.

Looking out of the window at all the parked Hondas and Toyotas lining the silent street, though only a few miles away, I knew I wasn't in Venice any more. The quiet was nice. Even if Derrick didn't come and live here, I would make this home. It might be nice to have my own space: no one telling me what to do; no one else to take care of. I could handle that.

The knock at the front door startled me. I quickly tiptoed across the small living room and looked to see who it was. I already knew, but I looked anyway, just in case. Through the peephole, his normally sharp features were round and exaggerated, and his face looked as if it was trapped in a fish bowl. With his brown skin and curly dark hair, most people never even knew he was mixed. But his nose shot out like a pointed arrow, and his sharply ridged cheekbones sank and gave way to a delicate yet precise jawline, whispering secrets of a 15-year-old Polish girl's unplanned pregnancy. I opened the door to greet him.

'So, this is your new crib,' he said as he walked past me.

'Yep. This is it.' I felt proud.

After I showed him around by the faint moonlight, I could not resist asking the question that had been nagging me ever since I signed the lease.

'So, have you decided what you're going to do?'

Even in the dark, I could see the muscles in his jaw tense. My newfound freedom was a damper on his.

'I don't know.'

'You know, I can't afford to keep helping you with your rent now that I have to pay my own... not to mention school. I'm starting college next semester and I am planning on taking a full load of classes in the evenings.' Even if I wanted to get a second job to keep paying his rent, there just weren't enough hours in the day between working full-time and going to school.

'I know. You don't have to tell me that.' His voice was edgy and annoyed.

That night, he didn't answer my question, but he slept beside me on the scratchy beige carpet.

Part of me wanted him to man up and start taking care of himself. But another part of me was terrified that if he did, I would lose him. What would happen if he didn't need me? Would he stop calling? Maybe it was I who needed him. I wasn't entirely sure that I knew how to make it without him. I had met him when I was 11. Looking back, I could hardly remember a time when he wasn't there: steady and constant; a known in the midst of unknowns. What would life even look like without him? I didn't want to know. He came and stayed the next night, too. And the next. One night I lay awake beside him on a makeshift bed of blankets, wondering and wondering. I hated not knowing.

'Are you staying?' I finally asked.

He didn't respond. It never occurred to me that it didn't have to be his choice; that power didn't always have to rest in a place outside myself.

A few days later, he asked if I could give him a ride to his place. He must already have received an eviction notice, because when we arrived, we snuck around like robbers and broke in through a window to retrieve his belongings. He brought his stuff to my apartment. That was his answer.

I sat on my broken futon, clipping coupons out of the Sunday paper. It was the main reason I bought the paper. I'd sift through all the tragedies and funnies and flip to the section with that bright shiny coupon paper. Entertaining the idea that Derrick would actually get a job, I glanced through the

Classifieds looking for something that didn't require much skill or education. And there it was. The same ad in bold print, bigger than all the others:

HOSTESS POSITIONS. GIRLS WANTED. $150–300 A NIGHT. 18 AND OLDER.

I was old enough. But it always seemed too good to be true. Just what would I have to do to make that much money? *If they are advertising in the* LA Times, *it can't be that bad… can it?* There was only one way to find out. So I dialed the number.

'Hi. I'm calling about the job…'

'Yeah. When do you want to come in for an interview?' a gruff female voice responded.

'Well, I actually wanted to know more about the position first.'

'This is a night club. We hire girls to entertain our customers.'

'Oh, I see…' I didn't see. 'What kind of entertainment?'

'Well, it all depends. Men come here to have a drink, play pool, dance. They like to be surrounded by beautiful women…'

'That's it?' I asked wearily.

'Yes. Would you like to come in for an interview tonight?'

I pictured an upscale nightclub where wealthy men on business came to spend some free time. In Hollywood, they let pretty girls into clubs for free, because 'men like to be surrounded by beautiful women'. Maybe this place just took it a step further and paid women to come to their club. I had nothing to lose, so I said yes. I put on a short, black, spaghetti-strapped sundress and asked Derrick to drive me to the interview. We pulled up in front of a seedy little spot in downtown Los Angeles with a neon sign.

'Are you sure this is the place?' I asked Derrick.

'This is the address you gave me,' he replied.

So much for upscale. Skid row was just around the corner. As I walked up to the door, there were men lurking and meandering aimlessly about the grey, littered streets. Climbing up the dark staircase to meet my potential employer, I felt thankful that Derrick was going to stay outside in the car until my interview was over.

I knocked on an unmarked, black door at the top of the staircase, and a heavy-set Mexican woman wearing a dull and jaded expression greeted me. She led me through the empty club to a small office with a view of the streets below. I wanted to look outside to make sure Derrick was still there. The woman looked at me with eyes that spoke of many that came before me and many that would come after me. She didn't ask to see a résumé. She didn't even ask me about previous job experience.

'You'll be paid by the minute for time spent with the clients. When a man chooses you, take this time card and use the time machine next to the couches to punch in,' she said, handing me a time card.

'Then what?' I asked, still not fully understanding why a man would pay by the minute to spend time with me. I couldn't figure out why they just didn't go to a regular club and buy women drinks like normal guys.

'Then you spend time with them,' she said, as though I should be getting it by now.

'That's it?' I probed.

'Yes. That's it.'

'They can't touch me, can they?'

'No. There's no touching allowed,' she said monotonously, as if she were reading it from a training manual. The set-up didn't sit well with me, but desperation for money made room for my uneasiness. I ran downstairs to tell Derrick I had been hired on the spot. He could pick me up at 2.00 am.

By the time I finished filling out the minimal paperwork asking for my name, address, date of birth and social security number, the club had opened and a small but steady stream of customers began to fill the place. I noticed a few men straggling around, right outside the office door. When the boss lady escorted me onto the floor, the straggling men followed closely, calling out to her in Spanish. They were asking for first dibs on me. I turned to see the painted faces of the women, sitting, bored, in satiny and glittery dresses, on a cluster of red velvet couches lining the outer edges of a dance floor. With jaded eyes, they looked me up and down as I walked towards them and reluctantly returned my smiles.

The boss lady bantered rapidly with the men that had followed us, until they figured out who would have the first turn with me.

'Punch here,' she said, pointing to the time machine. Then she motioned for me to scoot along, and she sent me off with a stout man with slick black hair combed back neatly.

There was something unsettling about the whole thing. My gut told me that these men expected much more than good company and conversation. I glanced back at the boss lady, hoping that she would recognize the fear on my face – hoping that there was a maternal instinct inside of her somewhere, and that she would call me back to the safety of her office. She remained stoic and hard, and I floundering and lost.

The man led me to a half-moon booth with a table. I looked around for other girls, but they were all sitting on the velvet couch waiting for someone to pay for their time. I had no idea what I was supposed to do next. I sat opposite him – as far away as possible. Ridiculously far.

'Come here. Come sit over here,' he said, in a subtle Mexican accent, as he patted the cushion next to him.

'No, thank you. I am fine right here,' I replied, looking around nervously.

He chuckled, and then proceeded to offer the first bit of advice I received regarding my new job. 'Listen, if you want to make any money in this place, you are going to have to be a little friendlier. You have to get a little touchy, if you know what I mean.'

I sat there in a silent stand-off, refusing to heed his advice. After a few moments, he slid towards me and put his hand on my leg. With a knee-jerk reaction, I pushed his hand away and marched straight over to the boss lady.

'That guy just touched me!'

'There is no touching allowed,' she replied mechanically.

There was already a small line of men formed, waiting for their piece of me. I began to feel like a supermarket special: 'Now on sale, fresh meat.' I saw the green exit sign and I wanted to follow it straight out of that place, but I had already come so far. Besides, Derrick wouldn't be back to pick me up for hours.

The next client was even more aggressive than the first, groping at me and pulling my hips towards his, despite my protests. I looked over to see another woman on the dance floor, doing much more than dancing with her client. I pulled myself from the man's grip and ran to the back office, where I demanded to use the phone to call my ride. At this point, the boss lady seemed glad to see me go.

While I was waiting for Derrick to pick me up, two women walked into the office seeking employment. They were beautiful, head-turners: the kind of women I had always admired. They looked as if they should be sipping champagne in some fancy restaurant on Sunset Boulevard.

'You guys don't belong here. This place is horrible! They

say there's no touching, but there really is. You should see what one of those girls is doing out there!' I warned them, as soon as the boss lady left the room.

They exchanged a glance and looked back at me. What was it in their eyes? Pity? Arrogance? Mockery? It certainly wasn't gratitude. They knew exactly where they were and what they were doing there. But why? Why would beautiful women like them choose to work in a place like that, I wondered.

I don't care how much money they pay me, I could never do it, I thought to myself.

When the phone rang, I lifted my heavy head to see the time. It was 6.00 am. I thought it was weird that someone would call that early. Derrick finally answered on the fourth ring. Though he was in the bed next to me, I could barely hear his tired muffled voice over the sound of the traffic outside our window on Overland Avenue.

Derrick shot up into a sitting position. His thick brown eyebrows were knit so tightly it almost looked like he had a unibrow.

'What? Are you serious?' He sounded panicked.

'Where is she?' he continued.

I sat up and mouthed the words 'Who is it?'

He threw the covers off and walked out of the room, leaving me wondering. When he returned to the bedroom, he began tugging clothes out of the closet.

'What's going on? Where are you going?' I asked.

'I have some things I have to take care of.'

'What kind of things? Derrick, tell me what's going on.' Urgency and desperation strained my voice.

He turned and looked me dead in the eye; his body was motionless and I froze too. Silence. I knew him well enough to realize that it was time to leave him alone. He showered and dressed while I waited on our futon couch in the living room. If I made myself visible, maybe he would change his mind about talking to me. When he had finished getting ready, he walked right past me and straight to the door without so much as looking in my direction. He stood with the doorknob in his hand and looked at me out of the corner of his eye.

'My mom had a stroke. I'm going to see her.'

Before I could say anything, he was gone.

I went to work that day and came home as fast as I could. When the ten o'clock news came on later that night, I was sitting on the black futon couch in the same exact place as when Derrick had left that morning. On the television screen, there were clips of the scene of a fatal car crash. The helicopter shot showed a freeway littered with fire engines and ambulances, and somewhere in the wreck of it all, there were dead bodies. Bodies of people with plans to be somewhere; with ideas on what kind of food they wanted for dinner that night and who they wanted to go home to. And none of that mattered, because they were dead and trapped inside twisted burning metal.

I imagined Derrick caught up in that wreckage. The thought of his death brought terror to my heart. Tears slid down my cheeks as I watched the news. I wondered what would happen to me if he died. Would I survive? Would I even be invited to his funeral? I had never even met his family. They would never know the depth of my love for him – our history together. That he was the one who had always been there for me: when my father left; when my mother left. When all I had to eat was tortillas with butter, he took me to the corner store and bought me and my brother food.

I imagined what my life would be like if Derrick never came back. I would have to kill myself – I would slice my wrists in the bathtub and watch life spill out of me. I knew I couldn't face living without him.

I heard the keys jiggle outside the door and I sat at full attention, waiting for him to enter. He walked in and didn't say anything. I sat still on the couch and watched him walk to the kitchen for a drink. He sat on the opposite end of the couch with a two-liter of soda in hand. I knew I shouldn't probe. Not wanting to say or do anything that would make him shut down, I waited silently until he spoke.

'She's paralyzed. She can't talk either. The doctors say she's gonna need live-in help. My sister has three kids, so she can't do it.'

There was so much restrained pain in his voice I wanted to comfort him, but he was never one to acknowledge vulnerability. 'Derricks don't lose,' he would say during a game of dominoes. 'Derricks don't get sick,' he would say, even as he blew his snotty nose. And most of all, 'Derricks don't cry.' He sat at the edge of the couch with his elbows resting on his knees, twisting the cap of the soda on and off. The sculpted muscles in his slender arms flexed with each movement.

'I told my sister I would do it, that I would move in and take care of her.'

My chest tightened at the thought of him leaving me, and I held my breath.

'I figure it'll be better to live in a house anyway. We'll have a yard,' he continued.

I quietly let out my bated breath. We. He wasn't leaving me. I was going with him.

That night, we went to Derrick's adoptive mother's house in Santa Monica. In the seven years I had known Derrick, it was the first time I set foot in his mother's home. He had always been afraid to introduce me to his mother. As I walked up the steps leading to the house, I remembered the story Derrick told me years ago about his mother chasing his friends off her porch with a shotgun, a scene that would have seemed more fitting on a farm in Texas than in the heavily populated city of Santa Monica.

Behind the black iron security door, there was another door with five deadbolts. Inside, the house was dark and smelled like a musty library. I heard whimpering, and remembered the dog Derrick had told me about. He called out her name as he walked in the door: 'Budda!'

Although Derrick had sold some drugs here and there as a kid, he had vowed to never take them, for fear he might become a crack addict like his mother. Still, he was fond of naming his pets after mind-altering substances. Budda was another name for weed. Next on his pet agenda were two rottweilers named Coke and Caine. We turned the corner and there, boarded up in the kitchen, with no food or water, was a black-and-white spotted pit bull terrier with her ribs protruding. Derrick hopped over the wood blocking the entrance and began petting Budda. Though weak and frail, Budda found the energy to wag her tail. She plopped onto the ground so he would rub her soft pink belly.

'You're hungry, huh? Oh, I bet you are.' Derrick surprised me by using the typical high-pitched voice people use when they talk to animals and children.

'She must be hungry. Moms was trapped in the house for two days before the paramedics came and took her to the hospital,' he said, while petting Budda's belly with long gentle strokes.

She appeared malnourished. From the look of her sunken eyes and the way her skin hung over her bones, it seemed that Budda had gone longer than a couple of days without food. After getting Budda food and water, we went our separate ways and surveyed the rest of the house. All the light bulbs seemed to be

40 watts or less, so even after turning on every light in the house, the place was still dim.

The spare bedroom was like nothing I had ever seen before. Furniture was piled so high with books it looked like something out of a Dr Seuss book. It seemed I could hardly walk through the clutter without a chair or a bookcase toppling on my head. Still, I was so curious to know more about the mysteries of Derrick's mother I took my chances and tiptoed about the mess. In the center of the ceiling was a single light bulb with a long metal cord attached. I pulled the cord to get a better view of my surroundings.

There was a desk pushed against the wall. On top of it, there was an old chair upholstered with deep burgundy fabric. On top of the chair was a pile of at least 50 dusty books with worn hardback covers. I leaned in close to read the labels. What kind of books did this woman spend her time reading?

The word *Witchcraft* was printed in faded gold lettering on the spine of one of the books. It was enough to make me spin around and run to other end of the house, where Derrick was. Breathless, I entered the master bedroom, to find Derrick pulling at the ends of thick, dark brown drapes, trying to dislodge them from the wall they were nailed to. Suddenly, I got the sense that someone was standing behind me. I turned quickly. There was no one there.

'What are you doing?' I let my voice ring out, loud and normal, to chase away the fear I felt coursing through my body.

'What does it look like I'm doing?' He stood on top of a chair to reach the top of the curtains.

I looked around the room, which was furnished with a mahogany, matching bedroom set complete with headboard, dressers and armoire. The bed was neatly made and looked as if it belonged in a catalogue. The bedspread and pillows were deep burgundy, with a fine paisley print.

'Why does she have her curtains all nailed up like that?' I asked.

He didn't answer me.

When he finally tugged the first curtain free, I expected to see windows looking out on the backyard. Instead, all I saw was unfinished pine. Derrick's mother was not satisfied with nailing her curtains to the wall; she took the extra measure of boarding up the windows. Either this woman was afraid of someone getting into the house, or she was trying to keep someone from getting out of the house. Both ideas were unsettling. I could only hope that our new residence was less creepy in the light of day.

The next weekend, we moved what little we owned into the quaint, two-bedroomed, possibly haunted house, a couple of miles away in Santa Monica.

The water in my bath was so hot it made me dizzy. Beads of sweat dripped into my eyes. I had always wanted to be the kind of woman who took leisurely baths. I had even lit a candle and turned on the radio to KJLH. The Isley Brothers were playing. I wanted to unwind, but the water was so scalding my skin itched.

Why did I make the bath so hot? I pushed through my discomfort, knowing the heat would eventually dissipate and I could relax. This was rather the way I approached life. I put up with pain in hopes that I could outlast it. I could feel my face throbbing from the heat.

What do people do in baths? How do people sit still this long with nothing to do? For three months I had been running myself ragged: between work and school and taking care of Derrick's paralyzed mother, there hadn't been time for stillness. No time to sit and think; I had preferred it that way, because thinking only made me sad. But in the end we realized that we couldn't care for her adequately. So we made the difficult decision that she needed to be in a nursing home with 24-hour care.

With Derrick's mother gone, now I had time to take an inventory of my life; time to notice the piling debt and the distance between Derrick and me. Since I didn't have to dart home from school and work to take care of her, there was a void in my schedule, and more time to try *not* to think.

Since we had moved in with her, Derrick and I were hardly in the house at the same time. As soon as I got home, Derrick would bolt out the door, relieved to get a break from his mother and her frequent attempts at escape. I spent all of my spare time tending to her every beck and grunt. 'Shlum Dem! Shlum Dem!' she cried out when she was hungry. 'Shlum Dem!' she called when she needed help getting from her wheelchair to the potty chair. After spending all day at my new job at the nursery school, changing stinky toddler diapers, I came home to the feces and urine of a 60-year-old untreated schizophrenic.

Now that she was gone, I hoped that Derrick and I would finally get to spend time together. We could linger in the park late at night, shooting hoops and laughing, like we used to.

The water in the bath began to cool. Marvin Gaye was singing 'I Heard It Through the Grapevine', and I leaned over to turn down the radio. Derrick had always prided himself on being a private person – not showing vulnerability; not allowing people, including me, to see his flaws and weaknesses. The first time I was given the tiniest glimpse into his personal life was when he showed up at my house when he was 15 and I was 13, with a neatly penciled letter in his hand.

'There are things about me you don't know. There are some things I can't tell you. I want to tell you but I can't. Here is a rap that will help you understand…' the letter read.

It ended with a rap that talked about growing up in the streets and slanging crack. I asked him if he wrote it, and he didn't respond. Whether he did or not, he was trying to tell me something about who he was in this world. I felt that he was showing me that no matter how much he wanted to be close to me, he couldn't. He wasn't capable. I wasn't hurt that he didn't open up more; I was honored that he wanted to.

It was these glimpses of his woundedness that gave me hope for our relationship. It gave me hope that I could foster a bond of dependency with him that would make it impossible for him to leave me. My mom said that she and I were healers. Wounded people need other people to repair them, and I needed someone to repair. I was determined to love Derrick until he was better – until *I* was better.

When I was little, my grandmother took me to visit some of our relations. These relations had a black rabbit named Lucy. But Lucy was unsocialized and completely afraid of people. Hearing this, I became determined to reach timid Lucy. I went to the backyard, where I found her huddled in the corner of a pile of wood, just out of reach. With rabbit pellets in my hand, I lay flat on the ground, quietly wooing her to me. I was determined to reach the unreachable; to show her that I was a safe person. In two hours, Lucy felt safe enough to eat out of my hand.

I wanted the same for Derrick. I wanted to show him that no matter how bitter and lonely the world could be, there was one person he could count on. And I was willing to stay there with my hand opened wide for as long as it took to prove it.

I extended my hand to him, giving him money and everything I thought he needed. He reluctantly accepted my offerings; only they didn't draw him closer to me, as they had with Lucy. Now that I had lived in his home with his mother and seen all the things that he had spent his life trying to hide and cover up, he wedged himself further into the corner, further out of reach.

The sound of the front door closing yanked me out of my thoughts. Was someone here? Maybe it was the neighbor, Terrance, and his girlfriend Gina.

The bathwater was starting to get cold, and I couldn't sit still any longer. Especially if we had guests. After drying off, I wrapped myself in a scruffy blue bath towel and peeked into the living room.

'Hello?'

The house was silent. No television. No voices.

'Hello?' I called out, a little louder.

Still no answer. It was ten o'clock at night. Derrick was gone. I looked outside, to see that my car was gone, too. Maybe he went to the store or something. Where else could he go at this hour? I put on my pajamas and sat on the couch, waiting. And waiting. Thirty minutes – an hour – still no Derrick. I was startled by a knock at the door, and tiptoed over to look through the peephole. It was Terrance, Derrick's childhood friend, who still lived in his mother's house next door.

'Hey!' I said, opening the door and welcoming him.

He shifted nervously.

'Hey... is Derrick here?'

'No. He left. I don't know where he is. I'll tell him you stopped by, though.'

I expected Terrance to leave, but he stood there silently. Processing.

'Gina's gone, too. She left about an hour ago.'

I wondered if they were together, then quickly told myself that Derrick wouldn't possibly do that to a friend. Would he? Terrance and I stood in the doorway, looking at each other helplessly. I invited him in. If we were going to sit around and wait for them to come home, we might as well do it together. We sat on opposite ends of the couch, an awkward silence between us. Were we supposed to talk about the fact that his childhood friend just took off with his girlfriend?

'Did Gina say where she was going?' I finally asked.

'No. We got into it, and she just left. I thought she would come right back, like she usually does…'

'What were you guys fighting about?' Was their fight about Derrick? Had something been going on between them and I was the last to know, I wondered.

Terrance seemed to contemplate his words. His skin was smooth, dark chocolate. His face was pretty, but his body was thick and muscular from years of playing football. He took a deep breath, lowered his eyes and answered.

'Actually, we were fighting about sex. She knows that I want to wait till I'm married, but she keeps pushing me.'

I didn't even try to hide my disbelief. 'You have to be kidding me! Are you serious?'

He looked up at me and I saw genuine hurt in his eyes. He was telling the truth. I had never heard a guy say this sort of thing. It just didn't make sense to me. Wasn't it supposed to be the other way around? Guys pressuring girls. Shouldn't he be happy that she wants to have sex with him?

'Gina thinks it's weird, too. She doesn't understand.'

'No… I mean, you know, I've never heard anything like that,' I stuttered, searching for words.

'My faith is really important to me. I try telling her that, but she doesn't get it.'

I didn't want to tell him that I didn't get it either. We both fell silent, looking at the television out of habit. It was off.

'Do you like gospel?'

'Yeah. Actually, I love gospel. I love the passion of it.'

'I'll run to my house and get a tape of my favorite songs for you. You can have it. My brother made copies.'

After a few minutes, he came back and dropped off the tape. I closed the door and went back to the couch with the tape in hand. What was I supposed to do? Just sit here all night waiting up for Derrick? Is that what he wanted? I wanted him to worry about me as much as he was making me worry about him. So I came up with a plan. I would walk to the little cottage that housed the nursery school where I worked, let myself in and hang out there as late as I could. Derrick was bound to come home to an empty house. Then he would know what it felt like not to know.

Clutching the cassette tape and my keys, I walked half a mile to the cottage and quietly snuck in, making sure none of the neighbors were watching. I kept all the lights off, so that no one would see me. By the light of the full moon I put Terrance's tape into the cassette player and lay by the French windows, looking at the indigo night sky.

'My voice is an instrument of praise,' a woman belted in a rich velvet voice.

Voice as an instrument. I liked that idea. If the voice is an instrument, it's my favorite one of all. Really great jazz singers can mimic the trumpet and the sax, and others can make their voices swell like the sound of a passing train. Yes, the voice is the greatest instrument. As I listened to the passionate riffs and runs of the gospel singers, I longed to have a voice.

When the tape ended, I played it again. And again, and again, until hours passed and the anxiety I felt about Derrick's disappearance dissipated. I started to doze off and decided to return home. The air was cooler now. I walked briskly, wishing I had brought a sweatshirt with me. Four homeless men standing outside of the liquor store made no apologies, staring at me as I passed. I felt very aware of my whiteness. Even though I wanted to glance at them to see if Derrick's older brother, who I knew was homeless, was among them, I kept my head forward and walked confidently, as though I belonged. It was the same walk I used growing up in the streets of Ghost Town in Venice.

Cold and tired, I made it home and immediately noticed that my car was still gone. I felt a sharp pang in my stomach. Derrick was still gone, too. The house was dark and empty. I crawled into bed, facing the bedroom door – waiting. Placing my head on the cool pillow, I gave in to tears. I cried quietly, but my body heaved and shook almost violently. If I allowed sound to escape, it would come in the form of wailing. Derrick was further away now than ever.

He didn't return that night. Or the next. Or the night after that. Each evening, when I returned from school to see that my car was still missing from the driveway, my heart filled with more despair. And then there was the anger. How could he leave me like this? How could he run off with someone else when I was the one taking care of him? I was the one who had just spent the past few months wiping his mother's behind, and he left me alone in her house the first chance he got! The feelings were more than I could bear – so I didn't. I pushed them right back down into my stomach, where they strung together in knots.

As soon as my English class was over, I shoved my books into my backpack, ready to race home. I was exhausted from staying up each night, wondering and worrying about where Derrick was, and all I could think about was getting back to see if he was home yet. Walking through the school hallway, I heard a voice call from behind.

'Harmony! Hey, Harmony, wait up.'

It was Evan from my class. All semester, he had been sitting next to me, trying to make small talk about whether or not I had done the reading, studied for the test, had a good weekend; anything he could think up to talk about. I stopped and waited for him to catch up. He pulled the straps of his backpack forward to tighten the slack as he hurried towards me.

'Hey, I just wanted to see what you were doing tonight. Wondering if you wanted to get a cup of coffee or something at The Coffee Bean.' Slightly overweight, he was out of breath from his short jaunt down the hall. A thick coif of ruddy hair was perched atop his head.

'Sorry. I don't drink coffee.'

'It's Coffee Bean. They have other stuff there. You can get tea or something.'

I had never been to The Coffee Bean. Never even heard of it. 'Yeah, no… thanks. I've been working all day and I should probably get home and do some reading.'

'Come on, you know you're already like a week ahead of the reading. Live a little!' My overzealous work ethic was no secret. I was actually *two* weeks ahead.

I figured it would be a good idea to get out of that house. It wouldn't do me any good to sit around all night worrying about what Derrick was doing.

'OK, fine. I'll go. But I can't stay out too late. I have to work in the morning.'

The Coffee Bean was packed full of 20-somethings dressed in designer jeans, chatting over espresso drinks and biscotti. I couldn't fathom why anyone would pay $3 for a coffee. It was beyond me. $3 could buy shampoo, conditioner *and* hair gel to last a month at the 99 cents store. It's a good thing Evan is buying, I thought.

A table opened up outside, and we sat, he with his coffee, I with my tea. He wanted to know about me. What was there to say? I work; I go to school; I study; I sleep a little; and now that I am not taking care of my boyfriend's crazy paralyzed mother, in my free-time, I try to make a failing relationship work. I told him the parts that I could.

'I work, I go to school, I study, I sleep a little, and then I do it all again.'

'Why do you work so hard?' he asked, with compassionate eyes. He tilted his oblong, freckled face to one side.

'What do you mean?' Why wouldn't I work hard? What else was there?

'It's just that most girls your age are having fun. Going to parties, enjoying their college years.'

'Well, I guess I'm not most girls. I *have* to work. And as a matter of fact, I am at the point that I am probably going to have to get a second job,' I said, pulling the tea bag out of my tea.

He opened his mouth and drew in a breath, as though he was going to say something; then changed his mind.

'What? What were you going to say?' I prompted.

'It's just that my mom has this friend. And she has a job where she makes really good money. I don't know if it's my place to say anything, but a pretty girl like you could make a killing doing what she does. You wouldn't have to work so hard.'

'What does she do?'

He paused and seemed to contemplate his words. 'She's… she's – um – a topless dancer.' Well, there's a pimp move for you. Take a girl out to tea and suggest she become a stripper.

'What? What do you mean? I should be a stripper?' I let him hear that I was offended at the mere suggestion.

'She's not nude or anything. Just topless.'

'Well, thanks, but I could never do that.' I shot him a look: the fierce one my mother uses when she has been wronged and with one glance makes you want to apologize for your very existence on the planet.

'I'm sorry, Harmony. I didn't mean to... I... I knew I shouldn't have said anything...' He hung his head. 'I was just trying to help.'

If he hadn't been so benign-looking – like a plump version of Richie Cunningham – I might have been more skeptical of his intentions. But he lived at home with his mother, who served him fresh, sugar-sprinkled strawberries and milk. A guy like that wasn't looking for a meal ticket. He was just looking for something to spice up his boring life.

But for the directions I gave him – 'turn right here; go straight' – the drive to my house was silent. As we turned the corner to the dead-end street Derrick's mother's house was on, my heart beat wildly in anticipation. I imagined him sitting at home, wondering where I had been. Did he check the drawers to see if my clothes were still there? Did he think I had it in me to leave him?

'Here it is – the one on the right,' I said, pointing to the peach, stuccoed bungalow I called home. The car was still gone. My knees felt too weak to carry me.

Derrick had never taken off like this before. The distance between us was widening. I needed to do something to keep him from leaving me – something to make me worth coming home to.

'How much?' I finally asked.

'Huh?' His mouth hung open slightly as he waited for clarification.

'You said your friend makes good money. How much does she make?'

'Um, I don't know exactly. At least two or three hundred a night.'

A couple hundred a night! I could make my entire month's salary in a few days!

'I still don't think I could do it,' I said, trying more to convince myself than him.

That night, I woke up to the sound of keys in the front door. I sat up quickly, straining to hear his footsteps in the front of the house. I wasn't about to hop out of bed and run to him, when he had left me like that. Now that he had made it home safely, my sadness turned to anger; rage swelled in my chest and my heart thumped wildly.

After 15 minutes, he still had not come into the bedroom, so I gave in. I tiptoed out to the living room, where I found him lying on the couch with a blanket draped over him. I stood silently in the doorway, trying to find the voice I longed to have. I wanted to remind him of our history; of growing up, when he took the bus to my house every day of the summer, just to be with me. I wanted him to remember a time when the power was shifted; when he used to want me more than I wanted him. I wanted to say something profound – something that would change him or me or both – but the words weren't there. He looked up at me momentarily and then turned to his side. In that moment, I knew that I was losing him. Something had to be done.

Never one for sleeping in, Derrick was sitting on the couch playing video games when I got up the next morning for my 7:30 am math class. More than anything, I wanted to confront him; to demand that he tell me where he had been for the last few days. But I knew that if I asked, he would never tell. He would rather have bamboo shoots shoved underneath his fingernails and go without food for weeks than give up information that someone else wanted. Plus, I knew in my gut that he had been with Gina, a suspicion that was confirmed when I looked outside – her car was suddenly back in its usual spot, parked outside Terrance's house next door.

'We have to move.' Derrick broke the silent tension between us.

'What? What do you mean? When?' I asked.

'Now that my mom is in the nursing home, my sister wants to sell the house to pay for the cost.'

His sister hadn't seemed worried about covering any costs until then. She had left it all to us – to me! I took a deep breath, keeping my anger where I always kept it – to myself.

'What are we going to do?' I asked earnestly.

Oh God! Was there still a 'we'? Or was this it for us?

'Move. That's what we are going to do. *Move*.' He was getting annoyed.

'OK. Then I will start looking for a place,' I offered.

We needed money fast.

Nineteen

'I don't know if we should go,' I said, pushing a grape around in a bowl of fruit salad.

'It's not like you have to audition tonight. We can just go and check it out. If you don't like it, don't do it.' Evan's eyebrows were pushed up into empathetic arches.

'Yeah. I guess you're right...'

I couldn't believe that Derrick was OK about my scouting out strip clubs with some other guy. I thought he would be jealous, but I guess some things mattered more than the leash he kept me on. He wanted money.

'Maybe you should have a glass of wine or something. Just to take the edge off,' Evan suggested.

'I'm not 21.'

'That's OK.'

'I don't really drink. And I don't like the taste of wine anyway,' I said, looking around the brightly lit diner. People were chewing down on the nightly special: lukewarm pork chops, frozen peas and mashed potatoes from a box. Nobody else was drinking.

'I know just the thing for you, if you don't like the taste of wine,' he said, raising his finger to catch the attention of our waitress. 'Can I have a glass of White Zinfandel, please?' After flashing his ID, he turned to me, 'It's like training wheels for wine. You'll like it 'cuz it's sweet. Just don't let the waitress see you drink it.'

The wine was sweet and fruity. It reminded me of the Strawberry Hill my friends and I used to pay homeless people to buy for us from the liquor store when we were in high school. I hadn't had any alcohol since high school and I could feel its effect immediately. As we pulled up to the topless club in Inglewood, my blood felt warm and thick, my heart a little less nervous. We stood in line behind a group of already drunk customers. When it was our turn, Evan took the lead.

'Hi. My friend is thinking of applying for a job here, so we just wanted to come check it out.'

'ID, please,' the bouncer said, looking past us as though surveying the parking lot. Over his shoulder I could see rows of men sitting on bar stools, watching intently as a curvy brunette swayed seductively on stage. A strand of pearls hung from her neck and swung from side to side between her bosom. Shakily, I handed the bouncer my ID.

'I'm sorry. You have to be 21 to come in here.'

'I thought it was 18,' Evan quickly countered.

'Nope: topless clubs are 21 and over. We serve liquor. You might want to try one of the totally nude clubs. Those are 18 and over,' he said, while continuing to check IDs and wave men past us into the club.

'Doesn't that seem backwards to you? The younger you are,

the more you have to show? It doesn't make any sense,' I said as we headed back to Evan's car. The flashing red lights of planes, coming and going, sparkled above us in the night sky.

'Oh, well. At least we tried.' Truthfully, I was relieved. Stripping was no longer an option.

'I know of a nude club down the street,' he suggested as he turned his car on.

'Evan, let's just head home. There's no way I'm dancing nude.'

'It's just around the corner. We might as well… as long as we're here anyway.'

I knew his motives weren't pure. He couldn't be so concerned with my personal finances that he was willing to chauffeur me around town to 'help' me find a job. He wanted to see me naked. Still, my desperation was greater than his.

'Fine. But I can tell you right now it won't fly. I'm not dancing nude.'

The room was glowing dim red. Walking in, I was overcome with the sweet musk of cigarettes and body spray. Girls in lingerie and bikinis sauntered about the room while men, like drones, scouted them with their eyes. Evan and I took a seat three rows back from the stage and were warmly greeted by curious girls.

'Are you here for a job?' a sweet smiling woman with waist-length blonde locks asked. Her chartreuse bikini top matched the sheer sarong draped around her waist. Though she was upwards of 30, her pigeon-toed stance gave her a child-like quality.

'Um. Not really. I mean… I guess I'm just checking it out… I don't know, though,' I stammered.

'Oh, how cute! She's nervous,' the blonde woman giggled to her friend. 'You should. You should work here,' she assured me. 'Don't you think so?' Again she addressed her friend, who was standing stoically, atop ridiculously tall platform heels. The woman curved the edges of her glossy lips into a slight smile and walked away.

The blonde woman looked at her friend, then back at me, before shifting her way of working. 'So… would you like a table dance? They're only fourteen dollars.' She placed her hands on top of mine and shot me a flirtatious look.

Heart pounding and face blushing, I said 'No… thank you, though.' I was as much embarrassed on her behalf as mine.

'Are you sure?' Evan offered.

'Yeah, I'm sure,' I said, shooting him a quick, cold look. His eagerness was becoming repulsive. He couldn't even try to play it cool.

For the next several days, I tried to maintain my position. 'I could never do that,' I assured myself, believing it less each time. I was alone in my sentiment. Evan was zealous about getting a shot at seeing me naked, and Derrick was quite keen on the money. 'If I were a girl, I'd do it.' 'Girls put themselves through college doing it all the time.' 'You could always quit if you don't like it.' Their rhetoric filled my head.

Derrick first realized he could sell me when I was 15 years old. We were walking down Lincoln Boulevard in Venice when it occurred to him.

'It's crazy,' he said, shaking his head.

'What's crazy?' I inquired.

'That every single person driving by stops to look at you. Even the women.'

'What are you talking about? That's not even true,' I argued.

'Come here. Just sit down and watch,' he said, leading me to a bus bench.

He was right. For some it was just a quick casual glance. For others it was a lingering stare. Car after car; with very few exceptions, people looked. A wave of nausea rose within me. What were they looking at? What was it about me that made them do this? I would have liked to think that it was beauty that turned their heads, but deep inside I knew it was something else: the dirty hidden secrets about things done in the dark. What drew them to me was an ugly burden to bear. Derrick didn't see it the same way.

'I could *sell* you,' he mused.

'What? What are you talking about?' I demanded.

'I could sell you.' He threw his head back and laughed heartily. 'Hey! Hey!' he called out to a man walking by. 'You wanna buy her?'

'Derrick! Shut up!' I said firmly, reaching out to cover his mouth. Still smiling, he grabbed my hand and shoved it down. His other hand shot up in the air and he pointed at my head.

'Anybody got a nickel?' He continued his sales pitch to bewildered passers by.

So that was my going rate. A nickel. Lest I forget, every once in a while, in random public places, Derrick would remind me of my value by calling out to strangers, 'Anybody got a nickel?'

It seemed that Derrick had been waiting for a chance to capitalize on me ever since. And now, with stripping on the horizon, this was his chance. The truth is, I didn't want to be sold. I needed a voice of reason: a neutral third party to serve as a sounding board. I knew just the person.

The last child had gone home for the day, and the cottage rang silent with the absence of shrieking toddlers. I made a concoction of Clorox and water and began wiping down all the surfaces, where plump toddler fingers had left miniature greasy fingerprints. I had come to love the way the overwhelming smell of bleach lingered in the air. While mopping all of the floors, I was careful not to let the bleach splash the legs of my baggy blue sweatpants. The place was clean – my work day over.

With some time to spare before my five o'clock psychology class, I nestled up in the reading corner on the child-sized foam couches. Even though I was already a week ahead of the assigned reading, I pulled out my textbook, eager to soak in everything the subject had to offer; eager to please Dr Stevenson.

Unlike my psychology teacher in high school, who was old and stern, Dr Stevenson was young and fresh-faced. Less than 30 years old, he was playful and engaging. He seemed the kind of teacher who would have liked to hang out with his students on the weekends if it were allowed. It wasn't. I found that out when a guy in the class invited Dr Stevenson to a party.

Though he wasn't physically my type – far too yuppie-looking – I found myself drawn to him. He was intelligent and ambitious, and during his lectures a passion rose up in him, making his eyes and skin glow warm and bright. He was in his element, which is the most attractive thing a man can be.

As was the case in all of my classes, I sat in the front row on the right-hand side. Front and center would have been too obvious. Staying to the right communicated that I was anxious to learn, but uninterested in being teacher's pet (although I am certain my classmates would disagree). If I knew the answer to a question, my hand shot up compulsively. And because I read every textbook from cover to cover, I usually knew the answers. Getting an 'A' was all the incentive I needed to study on my lunch breaks and into the late hours of the night, but gaining favor in the eyes of Dr Stevenson was an added bonus.

On this particular afternoon, as I sat in the reading nook at the cottage, I found it difficult to focus on my studies. All I could think about was the conversation I would have with Dr Stevenson at the end of class, provided he would agree to see me.

He was my last chance of escaping stripping.

When I talked to Derrick about it, he slyly made out that he was leaving the decision in my hands.

'I just don't know what I should do. I don't know if I could do it,' I explained.

'It's up to you. I bet you could make a lot of money though. We could finally pay off some of these bills. And I could get the new Jordan's,' he added, wearing the charming boyish smile he used when he wanted something from me. And somehow, what I always heard was 'I need you'. This was the thread between us, holding us together. I reflected on the weight of it all for a moment, and then remembered the stakes.

'Yeah, but don't you think it would be weird for me to be naked in front of other men?'

'Like I said, it's up to you. If I were a girl I would do it,' he reasoned.

'But what about my career?' The idea of having 'a career', though vague and distant, had always been my Plan A. I didn't know much about what it would look like; only that I would spend my evenings relaxing on a long, black leather couch in my luxury high-rise apartment, sipping white wine and enjoying a dazzling view of downtown Los Angeles with Miles Davis playing on the stereo.

My career was how I planned to escape the grip of poverty and make sure that no landlord ever had the power to put me out on the streets. And while all these other girls Derrick had been dealing with were stuck in dead-end jobs working at Footlocker and the like, I would have a real job that paid real money. Surely he would choose me then.

Derrick hadn't answered my question.

'Derrick, what about my career? What if it ruins my chances of being a child psychologist?'

'I don't know what to tell you.' His tone indicated that it was a price I just might have to pay.

'Maybe I should ask my teacher what he thinks. Maybe he can tell me what to do.'

'If you want to...' he said, sticking to his tactic of making it look as if I retained some sort of control over my own life. We both knew that I had already relinquished it all to him.

I got up from the reading corner and headed to the bathroom to freshen up and change, exchanging sweats and XL T-shirt for a thigh-high, floral-patterned tank dress that cinched at the waist. Whatever attention from Dr Stevenson I couldn't glean with my intellect, I was determined to win with my cutest outfit. I pulled the hair tie from out of my hair, smoothed out any stray strands by running my palms tightly over my head, and re-secured my ponytail. Final touch: a pair of black clogs my grandmother had bought me.

When class ended, my knees tingled, and before I could talk myself out of requesting a meeting, I practically leapt out of my seat and walked over to his desk. A line of students had already started forming. Everyone wanted to talk to him after class. Just weeks ago, I stood in the same line after his lecture on schizophrenia. The 'paranoid type' described Derrick's adoptive mother perfectly. The boarded-up windows; the curtains nailed to the wall; multiple deadbolts on each door because of all of the people 'out to get her'. Since her stroke, she had been unable to speak, but that didn't stop the ranting and groaning, 'Shlum Dem! Shlum Dem!'

At one point she called out to me, 'Shlum Dem...' It was a whimper: the small cry of someone who needs compassion. I held her hand, the one with feeling and movement, in mine. Her skin was thick and taut chocolate brown. I noticed her overgrown nails. Her face, the half of it that still had expression, spread into a smile when I began to file and paint her nails. Then, suddenly, she grabbed my arm with more strength than I ever expected she had and pulled me towards her. Her breath was sour and warm on my face. 'Shlum Dem!' she said through a clenched jaw. Her mouth could not form the words, but I sensed she was saying: 'Listen, white girl, you may wipe my behind and fix my meals, but I am still in charge around here.'

Throughout the night, she cried and moaned and threw herself out of bed, dragging her limp body to the door, where she would claw and scrape at the wood until we got up to help her. When I walked into the room, she would point at people and things that only she could see with such fear in her eyes that you might have thought she was looking at the devil himself. Talking to Dr Stevenson about her bizarre behavior made me feel less frightened. Dr Stevenson assured me that Derrick's mother wasn't possessed; she had a diagnosable disorder. I had questions; he had answers. I was comforted by him.

When the student in front of me finally finished talking to Dr Stevenson about this or that person in their family that had struggled with depression, I moved forward to speak with him. His shirt and slacks were neatly ironed and he smelled like dryer sheets. I hope I don't smell like children's Play Dough, I thought to myself.

'Hey, I was wondering if I could talk to you for a minute. I wanted to ask you something… in private.' I tried to appear calm and confident, but my voice came out soft and shaky.

'Sure. We can head over to my office after I finish here.'

His office was cluttered with books and papers. The fluorescent lights cast a green hue on everything in the tiny room. I had imagined that he would sit behind a big oak desk with a name plaque placed carefully at the edge, not this metal thing littered with yellow stick-on notes. It rattled every time he opened a drawer. He leaned comfortably into his leather office chair, and I sat straight and rigid with my hands in my lap in the chair across from him.

'So, what did you want to talk to me about?' he asked.

'Well. I really need some advice on something. You remember when I came to talk to you about my boyfriend's mother?'

'Yes, I remember, the one with schizophrenia.'

'Well, ever since I have been taking care of her, things have been really tough financially.' If Derrick would get a job, we would probably be just fine. And even though his mother had already moved out, supporting a sick woman sounded nobler than supporting an able-bodied guy without a job.

'So, I need to come up with another way to make money,' I continued. 'I love my job with the kids, but it doesn't pay enough. So…' Afraid to look at him, I studied the tiny little flower pattern at the hem of my dress. *What will he think of me when I tell him what I am considering?*

'Well, my friend said that I should get a job as a stripper, but I just don't know…'

OK, Dr Stevenson, this is where you interrupt me and tell me that a sweet girl like me shouldn't have to resort to that sort of work. This is where you tell me that there must be some other option, that I have a bright future in front of me – one that doesn't include this.

He was silent. I looked up to see him with his chin resting on his fingers, as though he was still waiting for what I had to say. *Maybe he didn't hear me.*

'So, what is it that you wanted to ask me about?' he said, shifting in his chair.

'Um. Well. That. I mean, you know I want to be a developmental psychologist, right? And I don't want to do anything that would have a negative impact on my career. I just don't know if stripping is a good idea, you know?'

'Well, it's not like you have to put it on your résumé.' He let out a little laugh as he said it, as if it wasn't a big deal. Maybe it wasn't.

'Yeah. I guess you're right. I just wanted to be sure. I mean, I would only do it for a couple of months, but I don't want it to come back and bite me.'

'So your friend suggested it to you?'

'Yeah. He knows someone who dances and she makes a lot of money.'

'Where?'

'Pardon?'

'What club are you thinking of working at?' The question struck me as odd. What did it matter 'what club'?

'It's right by LAX.'

Two
SCARRED

UNTIL THE PAIN OF REMAINING THE SAME HURTS MORE THAN
THE PAIN OF CHANGE, MOST PEOPLE PREFER TO REMAIN THE
SAME.

Dr Richard D. Dobbins

I sat in the passenger seat of Evan's dark blue Toyota Camry. Looking past the tacky strip-club sign written in 1970s-style red and orange letters, I noticed in the distance a plane headed for LAX. Watching it fly through the night sky, I remembered a story my grandmother always told me. She came to visit me in the apartment we humorously called the Roach Motel in Venice, when I was two years old. She was a polished woman, with a self-made bundle of wealth from antique dealing and real-estate savvy, so seeing her one and only granddaughter live in such meager conditions tugged at her heart and pride. With tears brimming in her eyes, my grandmother would recount the story.

'We were walking hand in hand down the Boardwalk when you looked right up into the sky and said, "Grandma, I just wish we could fly away." I just wanted to take you away from that place,' she said, in her repressed southern accent. That accent gave away her Winnsboro, Texas, country-bumpkin roots, where city folk looked down on her cotton-picking country folk. She could no more shake that accent than she could her habit of pretending that everything was just fine when it wasn't. It was her pretending that made it possible *not* to take me away.

A passing jet sent vibrations through Evan's car. I have heard that the majority of a plane's fuel supply is used during take-off, because it takes so much energy to propel it into flight. On that night, sitting in the parking lot of the strip club, I was out of fuel. I had been working full-time; going to school full-time; had been taking care of Derrick's paralyzed, wheelchair-bound, paranoid schizophrenic mother; and was on the brink of bankruptcy; and meanwhile Derrick disappeared for days at a time with one girl or another. My self-esteem had been chiseled down to nothing, and I was losing every battle there was to fight. It seemed that the only thing I had going for me was my 4.0 grade point average, and even that was taking all the energy I had just to maintain. Another jet roared above our heads.

No, flight was not an option for me. The best I could do was to try to keep from crashing. I hoped that stripping would help me do that. I would be able to pay off my debt, and hopefully Derrick, who was more interested in spending time with the person with the most disposable income, would stop running off with other girls.

Evan's voice shook me out of my daze. 'Harmony, do you want me to go in with you?' I turned, to see a feigned look of concern, and I couldn't help getting annoyed that he would mask his own agenda to see me naked with a forged care for my well-being.

'No, I don't want you to go in with me,' I said, rolling my eyes. 'Let me make this clear: I don't *ever* want you to go in there while I am working, do you understand?'

'OK; I just didn't know if you needed my support.'

'No, I don't need your support, thank you. You'll be here at 2.00 am to pick me up, right?'

For a moment I felt sorry for him. The poor guy had to schlep me all around town, and there was really nothing in it for him. And Derrick! Here I am getting ready to work in a strip club to make money for the car he drives and the roof over his head, and he can't even be inconvenienced to give me a ride in my own car!

As soon as these thoughts came into my head I had to fight them off. They were pointless. If I brought up my feelings with Derrick, things would only get worse. He would silently punish me by spending even less time with me than he already did. If I ever wanted to gain his affection and devotion, I couldn't afford to make moves that would push him away. I knew that there was a game being played, and I was determined to win. My strategy: to be the last woman standing. Eventually, as all the other women disappeared, he would be left with me. And he would finally see that *I* was the one he could trust and lean on; the one who would always be there for him and take care of him. Yes; my love would win.

'Yeah; I'll be here at 2.00,' Evan replied.

I remembered the night of my audition. My heart was pounding so hard I thought it would escape my chest. I followed the manager to an empty room with a small stage in the middle. I could hear the muffled sounds of Prince singing 'Purple Rain' coming from the next room, where a woman was dancing on the main stage. She seemed light years away. I am different. I won't let myself become like them, I told myself.

Backstage, half hoping I wouldn't get the job, I peeled off the white cotton dress I was wearing and undressed my adolescent body. Taking one last glance in the mirror, I can remember looking myself in the eye and wondering who I was. Then I pulled back the curtain, stepped on the stage and made my way to the closest pole, gripping it firmly. It was the only thing keeping me from fainting. The manager called out my name and told me I could stop. Based on my knock-kneed performance, I was certain that he wouldn't hire me. I was wrong: I had the job. Suddenly, the woman in the next room wasn't so far away.

As I reached for the door handle of Evan's car, nervousness overwhelmed me. At the thought of dancing naked in front of strangers, I sucked in my stomach and ran my hand down my abdomen, wishing I had skipped breakfast as well as lunch so I would look thinner. Though I was 5 foot 8 inches and 125 pounds, I heard the voice that had been in my head since childhood: a voice that seemed to contradict the praise of men and the attention I received. It was still louder than any other. 'You are fat and ugly,' it snarled to my heart.

The idea of having to dance as though I thought I was sexy made my knees weak. As a girl, dance was my hobby. I performed jazz, lyrical and hip-hop routines at school assemblies and pep rallies, but none of that would help me tonight. This was a whole new world and an entirely different stage; one that I knew nothing of. I could only hope that the afternoon I had spent in my apartment with the curtains drawn, practicing the moves I had seen the other dancers do, would help me. That somehow I would not make a fool of myself.

With so much at stake in my life, failing to show up for this, my first shift, was not an option I had given myself. Still, I hesitated before getting out of the car.

'You'll be fine, Harmony,' Evan assured me.

A tall man wearing a navy blue windbreaker labeled 'Security' approached me as I stepped out of the car. His skin was ash-black and leathery, as though he had stood in parking lots on many days and nights, through the dry heat of Los Angeles summers and the chill of winter nights.

He looked up at me with eyes that drooped with age and experience 'Are you here to work?' he asked me as he scanned the rest of the parking lot.

'Yeah, it's my first night,' I said, smiling politely. He nodded slightly and looked off at a bus passing by, as though it was more engaging than my last statement. I imagined that he had stood in this concrete lot and watched thousands of girls like me come and go. Even though he was well beyond the point of caring about names, I figured everyone's a friend until they're not, so I introduced myself.

'I'm Harmony, by the way…'

'Jerome… All right, the girls enter through here,' he led me down a small walkway lined with two large, green trash dumpsters. No red carpet. Not even an attempt at elegance here. These girls have to walk by smelly garbage every night. I just hope none of them have ever ended up inside of one of those dumpsters.

He escorted me through the back door to the club and brought me down a hallway that looked as if it belonged in a hospital. The floors were cream-colored linoleum, the walls mute and bare.

'Wait right here while I get the manager,' Jerome said once we reached the end of the hall. I heard a toilet flush and watched a girl in a siren-red, patent-leather dress step out of a stall in the bathroom to my right. She stopped at a mirror, where she pursed her glossy lips and fluffed the roots of her platinum hair. When she finished, she walked directly past me, not even acknowledging my presence. I supposed it wasn't the type of place you come to make friends.

The dressing room smelled like a potpourri of Victoria's Secret body spray and it bustled with the sound of blow-dryers and chatting girls. Staying out of the doorframe, hoping that they wouldn't see me, I nervously tugged at the bottom of my argyle-patterned dress.

I was the new girl, ignorant of the ways of the business. Though my life was filled with them, I never liked unknowns, and everything about this place was unknown to me. I knew nothing of its operations or etiquette and felt completely out of place. The next day, I would be back in my comfort zone, working with the toddlers at the high-school teen parenting program. I took every child development class Santa Monica College had to offer, and if there was one thing I knew, it was toddlers. If only it paid more!

'Oooooh! A new girl...' I heard someone say, as much for my ears as the ears of those around her. I didn't know how I was supposed to respond. I wasn't sure if I should turn and introduce myself, so I played it safe and pretended I didn't hear her.

'Hey, new girl... what's your name?' Her voice rang with learned sweetness.

I turned to see a stunning woman with long, bone-straight black hair cascading down her back. She was encircled by three other girls, who looked at her with adoration. The other women in the room fell silent, as if waiting to see what she would do next.

'Harmony. What's yours?' I asked, smiling with as much confidence as I could.

'I'm Lotus... Look at you; you're so young! How old are you?' Her eyes filled with smoky lust as she looked me up and down.

'I'm 19.'

To my relief, the manager, Gabe, walked in. He seemed to notice my discomfort, and surveyed the dressing room to see Lotus with a sultry smirk on her face. Her red lips curved gently at the corners and her brows rose. Gabe turned to me with his kind and freckled face. His eyelashes were pale and feathery.

'Hey, sorry to keep you waiting. I'll give you a tour before you change. This is one of three locker rooms,' he said, pointing to the room where Lotus and her harem were sitting.

'Over here is a bathroom... it leads to the entrance to the

main stage. That's where you will go when it's time for your set.'

'Gabe, the new girl is cute, don't you think? I wonder if she likes women,' Lotus said, taunting seductively. The rest of the girls giggled.

I felt a hot flush come over me, and I was sure my face blushed red. I had a sense that her comments were more for the sake of her audience than a genuine interest in me. I tried to act normally, as if I was used to gorgeous half-naked women coming on to me. Gabe shook his head and grinned at Lotus the way a person would if they caught a five-year-old doing something devilish yet amusing, like putting a cat in a frilly dress.

'Come on, Harmony, I'll show you the rest of the place.'

Gabe pushed through a restaurant-style swinging door with circular windows, and a waft of smoke hit my face. I tried to hold my breath at first, but gave in when I realized the entire room was filled with thick, grey air. Casually, I drew my finger across my nose to block the smoke.

'That's the main stage, there,' he said, pointing to a large stage with black floors, surrounded by brass poles. Half of the 20 chairs surrounding the stage were filled with men sipping on non-alcoholic beverages, puffing on cigarettes, watching with intense stares.

Their focus was a thin, ghostly woman with jet-black hair. She was spiraling limply around a brass pole, using her right arm to support the weight of her knobby body.

'Over there are the table-dance booths,' Gabe said, pointing to a wall filled with cubicle-like booths, lined up like horse stalls. Each one contained a chair facing a table, overlooking a raised platform no bigger than six square feet. The thought of taking my clothes off for a stranger at such close quarters sent nervous tingles through my legs.

I noticed that all the other girls had cute little G-string tan lines and evenly tanned tushies. I, on the other hand, had a lily-white behind that stood in stark contrast to my deep golden skin. I had never even considered wearing a thong to the beach! Real cute, I thought. My butt was probably glowing in the dark under the black lights.

Gabe continued filling me in on all the details of the club like a Universal Studios tram guide. 'All the clubs in LA have lap dances. We used to have them too, but we lost our license. Long story. Anyway, so we just have the table dances. And some girls like 'em better anyway, 'cuz there's no contact with the customer. Well, that's the rule, anyway,' he said, chuckling.

'Over here is the DJ,' he said, escorting me to a booth at the back wall of the club nestled at the edge of a row of table-dance booths. 'And this is Doug, the DJ.'

I looked up to see a middle-aged man with shoulder-length, frizzy brown hair. A large purple birthmark covered the majority of his face. I wondered if it wore down his self-esteem to be such an unsightly man. He was surrounded by beautiful women who would never want him. At first, I felt sorry for him, but the moment he addressed me, I knew for certain that Doug was not some pity case. He looked at me and through me and tried to see more of me than I was comfortable showing and said, 'Well, well, well, look what we have here. Who is this pretty lady?'

'This is Harmony. It's her first time.' Gabe appeared accustomed to Doug's wiles.

Doug threw his head back and looked to the heavens as if to thank God. A cheesy smile spread across his purple face. 'I see. A virgin, if you will. How old are you, my darling?' he said in a deep voice.

I glanced at Gabe, who didn't seem fazed. Was I just supposed to stand back and allow this perverted older man to go on and on like this? I defaulted to sweetness.

'I'm 19,' I said, as kindly as I could. No sense getting fired on my first night.

'Nineteen years old! A baby and a virgin! The customers are going to *love* you. You're still a teenager, for God's sake! Make sure you tell them that; it will make you a lot of money around here.'

I looked at the room around me and noticed a few men lingering and watching me unashamedly. As much as it sickened me, I knew that Doug was right. If I was going to sell myself, that would have to be my brand: the young, innocent virgin. I figured I could tolerate that for a few months while I got my finances back into shape. Then I could drop this job and go back to singing Barney songs to two-year-olds.

'If you'll excuse me for a moment,' Doug said, drawing a microphone to his smirking face. 'Upon the main stage, the lovely young lady, Angel,' he said in a deep radio voice. 'Only fourteeeeen dollars for your own private table dance. Fourteeeeeen dollars…' His voice trailed off.

'So, Miss Harmony, I am going to add you to the rotation. Is that going to be your stage name?' Doug asked.

It seemed so phony to give myself some stripper name. I didn't want to be Bambi or Bubbles or something dumb like that.

'I guess so. I can just use Harmony as my stage name.'

'Harmony it is,' he said as he turned to a dry-erase board at the back of the booth. I watched him uncap a black marker and write H-A-R-M-O-N-Y on the board.

I felt the muscles in my neck and shoulders tighten. Seeing my name there in black and white was unsettling. I resisted the urge to climb over the DJ booth and frantically erase myself from the board – from this place. I didn't have it in me to work here. It couldn't be Harmony; it had to be someone else.

'OK, never mind. Can you please erase that?' I said, trying to remain collected. 'I will be Monique.' *Monique*: it's French – sexy, yet classy – and not too strippery.

'Mowneeek,' he said, letting the name roll along his tongue.

In one sweeping motion, he ran the eraser across the white plastic board and removed HARMONY. In its place, he wrote MONIQUE. I felt relieved. Monique it was. I would have to keep reminding myself not to slip up and tell anyone my real name when they asked. I followed Gabe across the floor to a dressing room located near a smaller side stage that was only used on busy nights.

'All right, this is where your locker will be. You can get changed in here.' He courteously knocked on the door twice before he opened it. There was a statuesque woman with a long, brown hair weave sitting in front of a small mirror. She was applying burgundy gloss to her lips. She glanced at us briefly, without moving her head, and resumed primping. As Gabe showed me which locker was mine, aware of my own make-up-less face, I ran my fingers across my lips. My make-up regime consisted of Chap Stick and mascara.

'I know it's small in here, but there aren't any lockers available in the larger dressing rooms,' he said apologetically. The room was shaped like a hallway and was only slightly bigger than most walk-in closets. I was relieved that I didn't have to change in front of Lotus and the other girls in her dressing room.

Gabe walked out of the room and left me standing alone with the girl at the mirror. I placed my Fredericks of Hollywood shopping bag and my purse in the chalky-pink locker and found myself staring inside, at the torn white remnants of stickers placed there by girls who had gone before me. I hoped that if

I stood there long enough, the girl at the mirror would leave the room and I could undress in private. She didn't. So I pulled the metallic gold cropped tank top and go-go shorts out of my bag. I didn't have any sexy outfits, and I certainly didn't have the money to buy one, so Evan offered to take me to buy my first stripper outfit. 'Here's the deal: I am going to get the least revealing outfit I can find. I figure I will show as little skin as possible,' I told him on the way to the mall.

I slipped into my new outfit as quickly as I could and then began to apply cherry-flavored Chap Stick, when my colleague spoke to me for the first time.

'You're not going to wear those shoes, are you?' she said with a look of dismay. I looked down at the worn black clogs my grandmother had bought me.

'Yeah, I am,' I replied with as much sureness as I could muster.

She sighed disapprovingly, smoothed the fly-aways from her weave and got up to leave the room. My heart raced with humiliation. I couldn't afford to buy new shoes until I made some money, and the clogs were the only heels of any sort I owned. At $60, they were also the most expensive shoes to ever grace my feet. I had cherished them from the moment my grandmother bought them for me.

Standing there with my unacceptable shoes, lycra get-up, and untanned butt, I, Harmony, felt so out of place that I wanted to walk right out of that club and never return. The thought of my insurmountable debt, the stack of bills on my kitchen counter, and the look I would see on Derrick's face if didn't bring home some money won over my pride, and I, Monique, opened the dressing room door and entered the club.

The moment I opened the door there was a man hovering around the dressing room, waiting for me: for my services. After exchanging formalities – Hi. How are you? Can I have a table dance? Yes – he followed me to the bar, where I borrowed some $5 tokens, since I didn't have the money to buy them yet.

'Tokens are the way that the house collects their money. Each time you do a dance, drop one of the $5 tokens in the machine to turn the lights in the table-dance booth on,' Gabe had explained.

The man and I walked over to the table-dance booths and I picked the first in the line-up, the one closest to the security guard. It also happened to be the one closest to Doug the DJ, and although I found him rather repelling, there was safety in numbers. If the customer tried to grope and grab at me like the men at the 'hostess club' where I worked for a total of 30 minutes before quitting, then I would have witnesses and possible interventionists.

The customer sat in his little chair, and I took my position on the platform on the opposite side of the table. When I turned to see Doug through the transparent plastic partition, he winked at me, a devilish smile spread across his face. I began to think it was worse to have him so close. Maybe he was the one I needed protecting from. I would have been better off in some dark corner where he couldn't see me.

A rock ballad I had never heard before began to play, and I wondered how I was supposed to dance to that kind of music. It sounded like a two-year-old banging pots and pans together and had no distinguishable beat. I glanced at the stage to get a glimpse of the dancer who had picked the song for her set and saw a surgery-enhanced blonde woman who appeared to be in her mid-thirties. With her itsy-bitsy nose, narrow hips, and DD silicon breasts, she reminded me of a Barbie doll.

I dropped a token into the machine. It was a metal box that looked like a coin collector for pony rides outside grocery stores. Red lights flooded the booth. When I glanced back at Doug, his lips pulled and twisted in exaggerated movements as he mouthed the word 'Teenager'. A wave of nausea passed over me. The customer sat at the edge of his chair and looked at me eagerly.

The song started and the lights were on, but I still wasn't sure how to do a table dance. I had only caught glimpses of other girls doing them from a distance. I peeked over at the girl in the booth next to me. She looked at her customer flirtatiously, her hips swaying in small figure eights as she reached behind her back to unhook her bra. I did my best to watch her out of the corner of my eye so I could mimic her movements, but within seconds, she was fully naked and ducked below the curtain and out of sight. I had not even taken off my top. I knew that I couldn't procrastinate any longer. In front of this man whose name I would never know, I stripped down to nakedness. My body stiffened and I hugged the back wall of the booth as I danced, making sure not to bend or shift into any revealing positions.

Vulnerable and exposed, I thought of Rudy Arias and the time I stood naked in the living room of my home with my hands covering my blushing face. I was 15 years old; he was in his 40s. He was a reputable photographer, who came highly recommended by one of my mother's friends. He was the only person in the modeling business that my mother trusted, and thus my only shot at a career of glamour and beauty.

Rudy told me that the only way I would ever be a successful model would be to get comfortable being naked. He was going to help me practice. My gut told me that it was just a sick ploy to see my body, but my dreams of becoming a supermodel kept me silent and compliant.

Dancing for the stranger in front of me reminded me of standing before Rudy that afternoon, desperate and exposed.

Rudy's next career advice was that I lose my virginity as soon as possible, so that I could become more comfortable with my sexuality. Not knowing that he was more than a year too late, benevolent man that he was, Rudy offered to help me put this into practice as well. One Sunday afternoon Rudy took me down to the Venice Boardwalk for inspiration, pointing out the girls with the 'it' factor as they walked by. They were head-turners: women who exuded sex and confidence and would never go unnoticed, he said. That is the kind of woman that he planned to shape me into. Until that day I never knew about 'it', or that I was missing 'it'. Rudy thought that I didn't have 'it' because I was still a virgin. I wondered why losing my virginity hadn't produced the coveted 'it'.

Did I have 'it' now, I wondered? Was that why this leering man was willing to pay to see me dance so awkwardly before him?

As part of his next ploy to pluck the flower that had already been plucked, Rudy took me out to the middle of the desert for a 'professional' photo shoot. As he pulled off the side of the highway and traveled for a mile or so down a dirt road to an abandoned shack, it occurred to me that I might never return. It was exactly how dumb girls died in movies. They went off with some strange, perverted man to a secluded location and got their heads chopped off. Thankfully, Rudy was more interested in nudity than violence. Instead of killing me, he had me pose naked in a sheer robe.

On the ride home that day, he stopped at a gas station. I was famished and dehydrated, but when he offered to buy me something from the mini-mart, I declined. I couldn't stand the thought of wanting or needing anything from him. When he hopped back in the car, he tossed a candy bar into my lap. He didn't buy me a candy bar because he cared about me, or the fact that I hadn't eaten all day; there was some other motive that I couldn't read. Whatever his reasoning, my instinct told me that by eating it, I would be giving up something: maybe the right to loathe him, or to be angry that he was taking advantage of the fact that my modeling career was in his hands. I held the candy bar in my lap for 30 minutes before hunger began to weaken my resolve. Shamefully, I surrendered and ate it.

And so, it was hunger that brought me to this point again: to a place where I was willing to sacrifice my pride and dignity to a deeper need. Only this time, my hunger was for the love of a man. I wouldn't even be there, dancing in the strip club, if it weren't for my insane fear of losing Derrick and the money I needed to keep him from leaving me for another.

The song finally ended, and I quickly picked up my skimpy outfit off the floor and pulled it to my chest in an effort to cover myself. To my surprise and dismay, the man asked for another dance. And another. At the end of three songs, he handed me $60 and walked away without asking for change. I accepted it without hesitation.

Sixty dollars! In ten minutes I had made more money than I had ever made in a day in my life. Of course, there were credit cards and a car note to be paid, but at this rate, at the end of the night I might just have enough money to go grocery shopping. I had been living off low-cost long-shelf-life items like Kool-Aid, Top Ramen, and potatoes for so long, I couldn't wait to buy string cheese and yogurt and real fruit juice. This was just the motivation I needed to dance for the other two men who were lined up waiting for their share of the teenager.

When Doug finally told me that I was next in the rotation to dance on stage, my heart sped and fluttered, and I could feel my body temperature rise. I couldn't imagine anything more terrifying than dancing naked in front of a room full of strangers.

Every blemish, every insecurity, laid bare for evaluation and critique. Everything I had ever tried to hide and cover with flattering clothing would be on display. I mean, isn't that everyone's worst nightmare: that they find themselves in a room full of people and everyone is dressed but them? Here I was, getting ready to immerse myself intentionally in a nightmarish experience; only I would never have the satisfaction of waking up in a cold sweat, reassuring myself that it never happened. It *was* happening... right then it was happening.

I stood in a small room and looked at myself in the full-length mirror, as I waited for a dancer to emerge from the black felt curtain leading to the stage, signifying the end of her set. The clogs really did look awkward, but short of going barefoot there was nothing I could do. I noticed the way the top of the go-go shorts pinched at my sides and felt self-loathing rise within me. When the dancer on stage emerged from the curtain, I moved forward to make my entrance.

'What the hell are you doing? You have to wait until I pick up my tips!' she barked as she tugged a schoolgirl skirt over her hips. She must have seen the confused look on my face, because she sighed heavily and took a less aggressive approach.

'You are not allowed to pick up your tips if you're still naked. You have to wait for me to come backstage, put my clothes on, pick up my tips, and then you can go,' she clarified.

As she picked up her tips, Doug the DJ did his monotonous spiel about $14 table dances.

'There, now it's your turn,' the other dancer said in a condescending tone as she exited the stage.

Before he began to play the first song I had selected for my set, Doug introduced me to the audience. 'Tonight for the first time on our stage, please welcome, the looooovely young lady Monique. Only nineteeeen years old, gentlemen, nineteeeeeeen years old,' his voice trailed.

'Insatiable' by Prince began to play. It was the sexiest song I knew, by the sexiest artist I knew, and I figured it might compensate for my lack of rehearsed sexiness. I knew enough from watching the other girls to drop my wallet near the wall at the back of the stage before I began to dance. As soon as I looked up, the room felt as though it was making circles around me. My only comfort was in the fact that for this, the first song, I could keep my clothes on, based on the house rules.

My head tingled and my body went numb with fear. I needed something to hold me up, something to stabilize me, and I saw my rescue in the form of a brass pole across the stage. As swiftly as I could, I made my way over and clutched it tightly. For the first half of the song, I danced ridiculously close to that one pole, making sure that it was never further than at arm's length. Smoke from the customers' cigarettes billowed around me like tiny curling smoke stacks, rising and dissipating, making the air thick and stale. Red and black lights blended together to create an illusion of flawlessness. Even the girls with cellulite and stretch marks looked good in those lights.

I did everything I could not to notice the customers. I focused on the glare of the stage lights and the exit sign at the back of the room, so I wouldn't see their faces. I did not bend and bow like the other girls, who grabbed their ankles and crawled on their hands and knees. I danced straight and poised; not to distinguish myself from them but out of a lack of practice. I had not been trained to dance in that way. The dance I was accustomed to doing was about technique and passion, communicating story and evoking emotion. This was altogether different.

When the DJ finally faded the song after three and a half minutes, I made a mad dash for the curtain. Knowing I would have to go back on stage totally nude, my heart raced and I couldn't bring my breathing back to a normal rhythm. Prince's song of the woman he met in a hotel lobby, 'Darling Nikki', began to play over the sound system as I peeled the gold material from my body, revealing my small, barely post-pubescent frame. Doug introduced me for the second time, beckoning me to the stage in a smooth, taunting voice.

'Please welcome, the lovely *young* lady… Moooooownique.'

I sucked in my stomach as hard as I could and entered the stage. Not even the brass pole could keep the room from toppling around me. My body trembled, making my movements awkward. I imagined every single customer getting get up and walking away from the stage and instantly felt even more humiliated.

I began to wish that they all *would* get up and leave. But they didn't. They leaned in hard and consumed me with their eyes, placing offerings of one-dollar bills at my feet; each bidding for a piece of me. In all of the newness of the situation, there was something oddly familiar about it. This was not the first time I had found myself exposed and trembling, the object of lusty eyes. I felt a cool numbing run through my body. I drifted away. Not physically; like so many times before, I began watching my life unfold and unravel from a distance, as if I were merely a bystander.

Despite the familiarity of it all, there was an element that was vastly different from the experiences of my past. There were no unwanted groping hands; no dominating threats insisting on submission and silence; no forceful entry. In that moment, surrounded by brass bars and distance, I felt as though *I* was in control. At end of my first shift, I left with $280. On the ride home, Evan asked me how my night was.

'It was fine,' I answered evasively.

All I could think about was the $280 in my wallet, and how I could make more money on my next shift. If I was going to take off my clothes for strangers for the next two months, then I was going to have to strategize as to how to make the most of it. I couldn't afford to waste any time lollygagging around; I was going to have to hustle.

That night, when I got home, I found Derrick waiting up for me on our second-hand, floral-patterned couch. The room was dark, but for the flickering blue light of the television.

'Hey,' I greeted him, and sat on the opposite end of the couch. I looked over and studied him for mood indicators. If he was in a bad mood, he would either ignore me or let out a sigh, telling me he didn't want me near him. If I was lucky and he wasn't in a funk, he would nod his head to acknowledge my presence, but his eyes would remain fixed on the television. If he was in a good mood...

'Hey, how'd it go?' He continued watching a re-run of *Family Matters*.

'It went OK.' I knew what he was getting at. He wanted to know how much money I had brought home. I wanted to make him ask.

'Really? That's cool.' There was silence for a few minutes as we both pretended to watch TV. 'How much money did you make?' he finally asked, looking at me for the first time since I walked in the door.

'$280.' I tried to act cool, like I expected to make that much.

'Really?' His eyes lit up and he began to smile. I loved that smile. I missed it. He pulled his fist to his face to cover his teeth and he let out a deep and controlled laugh. 'Man, if I were a girl, I'd be a stripper!'

I am not sure that I believed him.

'What are you gonna do with the money?' he asked.

'I don't know. I was thinking we could start to pay down some of the credit cards. Maybe go grocery shopping tomorrow.'

'Mmmm,' he said, reflectively – strategizing. 'You know I need some new basketball shoes, right?'

'I thought you just got new shoes.' I had to tread lightly. One wrong move and the conversation would be over and I would get the silent treatment, until I groveled and apologized for whatever 'offense' I had committed. And of course, the apology would probably have to include the $120 shoes *and* a new pair of basketball shorts.

'I got those shoes, like, a month ago. You know they're already worn out by now.'

Of course his shoes were worn out. While the rest of the world was at work, he played pick-up games at the park at least five days a week, five hours a day. Still, he 'needed' something from me and I had carved out my place in his life as the one he could need. Without that, there was nothing. I pulled out my wallet and handed him half of the money I made that night.

'Thank you,' he said sincerely, looking me in the eye. And that was my reward.

When my alarm went off at 6.00 am, my muscles were sore and tender, and I had blisters on the top of my feet where the edge of my clogs had rubbed my skin raw. I could feel the veins in my temples thrusting blood into my aching head. When I tried to swallow, it felt as though sandpaper was pushing its way down my throat. I tried to break loose a glob of post-nasal phlegm by snorting. I ran to the bathroom, as a slimy mass began to slip down the back of my throat, and spit out a black chunk of coagulated mucus.

Disgusting! And I wasn't even smoking! The words from an anti-tobacco campaign formed in my head: 'Second-hand smoke kills.' Derrick was still sleeping, so I tried to be as quiet as possible as I threw on the navy blue cut-off sweat pants and a plain grey swap-meet T-shirt.

'You should really do something about that,' I heard his groggy voice trail from the bed.

'Huh?'

'That's nasty…' He said it as though someone had stuck a rotten pickle under his nose.

'I know. It's from all that smoke last night.'

'No; not that. You need to work on the back of your legs.' He flipped over and pulled the covers over his head.

I twisted my body to look at myself from behind and closely examined the flaw I had never noticed. Perhaps I had spent so much time focusing on how much I hated my stomach that I had neglected to dislike my legs as much as I should have. Funny; I had always thought that they were my best feature, the one thing I didn't have to worry about fixing. Leave it to Derrick to help me find new things to be insecure about. I guess they did use to be in better shape, I thought, examining the faintly forming cellulite underneath my skin. When I went downstairs, Evan was already waiting outside for me, with a McDonald's bag sitting in the passenger seat and a cup of orange juice in the cup holder.

'Thanks.' I could feel the heat from the still-warm, meatless Egg McMuffin as I took the paper bag into my hands.

'You're welcome,' he said in a syrupy, sincere voice. His top lip curved over his bottom lip like a nasty turtle, and I realized that I wanted to punch him in the mouth.

If it weren't for him bringing me breakfast in the morning, I would be eating the food sent over from the high-school cafeteria for the toddlers: leftover waxy, red apples and stale, cold, scrambled eggs that tasted vaguely like cleaning supplies. Still, each time he gave me a ride, or drove from his house to bring me frozen yogurt for dinner when I craved it, I felt more indebted to him.

It had started out like all the others: periodic acts of kindness intended to win my affection. That was OK, enjoyable even, but with Evan, need-meeting had become something of a routine, and I knew he delighted in my growing dependency on him. I had worked all of my life to get to a place where I wouldn't have to rely on anyone for anything, and Evan chiseled away at my progress with a slow and creeping sabotage. *That* is why I felt like socking him in the mouth on this particular morning.

'So…' He wanted details about my first shift.

'So…' I mimicked him.

'How are you?' he asked. That's not what he really cared about.

'Fine,' I said, rolling my eyes and letting my annoyance with him seep into my words.

'All right; I was just checking.' He backed off.

The air between us grew thick and distant: the rest of the ride to my day job, silent. I could see in his hopeless eyes that he knew I was pulling away from him. As we drove westbound on the 10 Freeway, I leaned my head against the window and watched the passing green exit signs.

How loathsome it is to feel needy. Is that why Derrick didn't look at me when I walked into a room? Why he yanked at the tiny fragments of self-esteem that I still had with a bitter combination of piercing words and neglect? Is that why he hid our relationship from the world and slept with other women who thought I was simply his childhood friend and room-mate? Was he ashamed? Not of me, but of himself, for the way he had grown to need me.

My brief consideration of this dilemma was halted by a mere conclusion: there was nothing that could be done without risking loss. I had already lost a father to alcohol and apathy. I had lost a slew of stepmothers to divorce and suicide. I had lost my childhood and innocence to abuse and drug addicts. I had lost friends and boyfriends. Most of all, I had lost hope, and even the hope of hoping. Loss was inevitable. But I would do nothing to engage loss and everything I could to avoid it.

We pulled up to the chain-link fence surrounding the small cottage and its grassy playground peppered with toys. I loved it there. I loved the way that everything made sense. There was not an item in that place that hadn't been carefully and thoughtfully included to enhance early childhood education. Digging for earthworms in the sand and singing 'Wheels on the Bus' with two-year-olds was safe. And in this safe place, I had stumbled across an opportunity to relive my own childhood.

Mornings there were my favorite part of the day. I stepped out of Evan's car into the cool, damp seaside air of Santa Monica and opened up the cottage. Thick rays of soft yellow light broke through the large windows of the converted two-bedroom home. No one was there, and the place still smelled of pine disinfectant and bleach from the prior day's cleaning. I stood in the center of what would have been a living room and pretended that the place was mine. I allowed the warmth of sunlight to envelop me and imagined myself as a sophisticated woman with a peaceful life. I pictured myself looking graceful and lovely in a fluffy white bathrobe. My husband had left for a full day's work, and when he returned, I would cook him an elegant candle-lit dinner: lasagna and sparkling apple cider.

I was jarred from my fantasy when I saw Tommy running towards the cottage. His 15-year-old mother trailed behind him with a black backpack slung over one of her shoulders. She wore a tight T-shirt and denim miniskirt. Her eyes were tired and her belly was thick and round, even two years after giving birth.

'Tommy Boy!' I exclaimed excitedly. His thick lashes sprang out like feathers and his little lips were delicate pink bows against his creamy skin.

'Howey!' he said confidently, mispronouncing my name as he threw himself into my arms. Harmony was difficult for most two-year-olds to pronounce, so I answered to all sorts of versions of my name, including Homny, Homity, and of course, Howey. Tommy looked me in the eye with a serious look and started the day by posing a question.

'Wheels on bus?' His voice was scratchy and deep from a long night's sleep.

'You want to sing "Wheels on the Bus"?' I reflected.

'Yeahhhh!!' he said, jumping up and down, landing in stomps on both feet.

'OK, Tommy, I'm going to go now.' His mother spoke with a gentle smile gracing her young moon face.

'Howey, "Wheels on Bus"!' Tommy demanded as his mother left for her first class of the day.

'Bye Mom! See you after school,' I said, on behalf of Tommy. 'The wheels on the bus go round and round, round and round, round and round, the wheels on the bus go round and round, all over town,' I sang.

And so my day began: sitting on the floor singing children's songs in a place that offered a stark contrast to the night before. Tommy wiggled with delight as I serenaded him. He looked at me with such admiration that a bystander might have thought I was an acclaimed singer. There is nothing like the pure and honest love of a child.

The lead teacher, Angela, arrived, a sturdy woman with tightly permed blonde hair and lashes that stuck together in thick, yet neatly separated, black clumps. I had a difficult time disguising my fatigue.

'Are you alright?' she asked, concerned.

'Yeah, I'm OK. I'm just tired.'

I avoided eye contact, pretending to supervise Tommy as he played with a red plastic fire engine, but I felt Angela hold her gaze. What would she think if she knew that I had spent the evening dancing naked for strangers in a strip club?

For the rest of the day, each time the children tried to get me to join them in a game of chase or hide and seek, I redirected them, instead engaging them in low-energy activities such as story-telling and painting. But when Angela suggested that we go on a walk, which entailed piling eight toddlers into what looked like an over-sized shopping cart, there was no redirecting my way out of it. And since I was 30 years her junior, my job was to push. My tired quads burned with each step, but I did my best to hide the pain. I don't know how long I can keep this up, I thought to myself.

Before my next shift at the strip club, I needed a new outfit. I figured that if I could make that much money walking around the floor not showing much skin, maybe I could make even more money with a more revealing outfit. I had only worn the gold outfit once, so I figured I would simply exchange it for a more suitable get-up. I washed it by hand, hung it to dry and threw it back into the plastic Fredericks of Hollywood bag. It wasn't until I was standing at the store register that I realized there was a problem.

I had already selected the item for exchange: a black fishnet G-string leotard. The cashier stood before me in a handsome black two-piece skirt suit with a lacy camisole underneath. I handed her the shopping bag.

'I would like to exchange this, please.'

'Was there a problem?' she asked.

'I didn't like the way it fit me.'

The lingering smell of cigarette smoke escaped as she opened the shopping bag. I had thought that washing it would cut the smell. I was wrong. The look on the cashier's face told me that she not only noticed the strong odor, but was thoroughly disgusted by it. My heart leapt into my throat. All I could do was stand there as still as possible and hope that she would finish the transaction quickly. The lady slowly pulled the shiny material from the bag, pinching it with her index finger and thumb as though it was a soiled rag. I was horrified. Just how does one explain lingerie that smells as though it has spent eight hours in a smoke-filled club? The saleswoman called her manager over to the register.

'Can we accept this as a return?' she asked, her hand, like a claw, releasing the outfit and allowing it to drop onto the counter. She looked at the manager with raised eyebrows, and the two of them had a conversation with their eyes about what a low-life piece of crap I must be.

'I guess so,' she said and then flashed me a forced, cheesy, customer-service smile.

I walked out of the store with my new outfit and their burning gaze on my back. I felt the way I used to feel walking down the halls of my new school, after Maurice gushed and gossiped about all the details of our expulsion. 'I got kicked out of school for having sex with Harmony in the auditorium,' he would brag to anyone who would listen.

We had heard the footsteps, so by the time the Dean and Vice Principal walked into the foray, we were dressed: disheveled, but dressed nonetheless. I had given up fighting Maurice. It wasn't even really rape any more; more like learned compliance. Defining it mattered even less to the school. They expelled us both. My reputation was written on the bathroom stalls: 'Harmony is a slut.'

As I walked through the Santa Monica mall, I felt the heaviness of that identity press deep into my heart. I was a girl with dirty secrets, a girl who did unthinkable things, things that other women, more decent than me, would never do.

Leaving the store didn't make the feeling go away. As I passed by fresh-faced, latte-laden mothers pushing toddlers in cushiony strollers, sophisticated shoppers in their designer shoes, and career women on their lunch breaks buying perfectly tailored designer suits, I knew that I did not belong. I felt myself sinking into a secret life, secluded from real people living real lives. They would never invite a person like me into their fancy homes in the Santa Monica Mountains. How appalling it would be if they knew that someone as detestable as me wanted to be a therapist to their children one day.

I stood near the bar, with a clear view of the main stage and the backs of all the gazing customers: some middle-aged and balding; others with youthful locks of hair. I wasn't quite sure how to approach the sea of heads and convince them to give me their money.

Only a few other women graced the floor, and they too stood idly. A girl I recognized from Lotus's harem approached me. Or rather, she walked towards me with purpose, as one who had been sent on a reconnaissance mission, and then positioned herself beside me.

'So what's your name again?' she asked.

'Monique.'

'I'm Lucy. I'm Lotus's sister.'

I turned to take inventory of any resemblance. Lucy's skin was pale; her eyes, though almond, were only slightly so, her face round and soft. She looked nothing like Lotus, with her brown skin, sharp eyes, and chiseled face. Lucy's Vietnamese accent was thick and prominent, Lotus's non-existent. *Sisters.* Unlikely story, I thought. She recognized my skepticism.

'We have different moms. Same dad,' she said, covering her tracks.

'Oh, I see.'

'So, you never worked at another club,' she probed, wearing a wide-eyed expression of curiosity.

'No. Never. I'm actually not going to be here very long. No more than two months. I just need to pay off some debts,' I said, guarding myself tightly, like a well-trained boxer.

The corners of her mouth lifted and she smiled knowingly. 'Mmm-hmm,' she agreed, and we both pretended to believe – ourselves and each other. She had been around long enough to know that nobody stays for 'just two months', and I was wise enough to know when shady motives were being hidden behind a friendly face.

Lotus slunk onto the main stage. Lucy turned to watch her and held a devoted stare. Only she was not alone. It was as if the entire room had sucked in a breath and refused to release it. The bartenders, security guards, and cocktail waitresses stopped what they were doing to watch Lotus slink onto the stage. She held them all in this suspended state, and it soon became clear to me why.

Taking hold of the brass pole, she masterfully contorted her body around it and gracefully slid up it. Steady and strong, her acrobatics superseded those of a professional gymnast, and her body seemed to defy the laws of gravity. Her lithe limbs were swinging and shooting out, swirling around with such delicacy and poise. During the time she was on stage, I was no longer in a strip club. I was standing in the middle of a gallery, gazing at a masterpiece. She was art in motion. Captivated and inspired, I decided that I too would infuse skill into my stage performance. Anything to make it something other than what it was: my body for sale.

After her performance, Lotus glided over to the bar, allowing the room one more opportunity to behold her beauty, before doing private and far less breathtaking nude dances for $14. I boldly seized the moment and approached the unapproachable.

'Wow! That was amazing. I have never seen anything like that. I would love to learn how to do that kind of pole work,' I said invitingly. Perhaps she would see some potential in me and decide to make me her protégée.

She locked eyes with me for a moment, reminding me of her dominance. Then she slowly turned away and looked at something more worthy than I, before delivering her response.

'You would fall and crack your head open.' Her voice spilled like black oil. I believe she meant to strike fear into my heart. That is what she meant to do; but she had inspired me all the more.

Determined to prove to myself and Lotus that I was capable of captivating an audience as she had, night after night, when the strip club closed, I stayed late to familiarize myself with those shiny brass poles. Clumsily at first, I spun and whipped myself about until my hands were callused and hurting. Shakily I set out to learn to hang upside-down using nothing but the grip of my thighs. My skin pinched and bruised, but that did not hinder my resolve.

Two months came and went. Excited about the money I was making, Derrick found more time to spend with me. When I wasn't working, we went on trips to the mall, and out to restaurants I had always wanted to eat at but could never afford. But working 60 hours a week and going to school full-time was exhausting. Something had to give. Soon enough, I asked my employer at the teen-parenting program for a sit-down, in which I gave my two weeks' notice. I traded my day job for trips to the nail salon and afternoons spent perfecting my tan lines. But for a tiny triangle at the base of my G-string, my skin was finally smooth, golden brown all over. No more glowing white tushie.

On stage, I began implementing my newfound talents on the pole. The higher I climbed, the more dangerous the tricks, the more enamored my audience became. These flamboyant shows of strength and agility were far more profitable and far less vulnerable than meandering around the big black stage aimlessly for two songs straight. Just as at school, where I hid behind textbook knowledge and straight As, at the strip club I learned to hide behind craft and skill.

The novelty of my newness wore off quickly. I was no longer a virgin to the stage or the table-dance booths, and men weren't lining up to see the new girl on her first shift. There were newer, younger girls all the time. Like Mandy from the Mid-West, fresh-faced and unjaded, with hopes of making it as an actress in Hollywood. People thought we were sisters; but that was before she started mainlining speed and her fleshy, youthful frame withered into thin skin draped over protruding bones. And after Mandy there were others. A steady procession of women came and went.

To keep up with the continual stream of competition, it wasn't enough just to have a great stage performance and the cutest outfits. To make money, I had to hustle. Growing up, I had learned how to sell my mother's crystals to sun-scorched tourists on Venice Beach, while my mom looked on with pride. The trick was to make the person think that they needed that crystal more than you needed their money. The principles were pretty much the same in the strip club.

Then, as a teen, I learned to con strangers into giving me money using sob stories of having to get home and having no bus fare. As a 15-year-old loitering and shoplifting in and around the Beverly Center, I was in no hurry to get home. Instead, I used the money for bean and cheese burritos at Taco Bell and trips to the movies. As long as you flashed your pearly-whites and looked as innocent as possible, most people would pull cash out of their wallets without hesitation. Again, the same was true in the strip club.

I didn't dilly-dally when I got off stage, or spend time primping in the dressing-room with the other girls. After each set, I made a beeline for my locker, changed out of my stage outfit into something that could be taken on and off quickly (usually a slip-on dress with no bra or panties to fool around with), sprayed myself with body spray, patted the sweat from my forehead, and hit the floor. The Chap Stick I carried in my wallet was all the additional primping I needed. Two minutes tops, and I was back to work, wearing my most confident smile.

'Hey, Monique, this guy wants a dance from you,' Lacey said, grabbing my hand and whisking me off to the table-dance booths. 'They're having a bachelor party,' she said, introducing me to a man in a powder-blue collared shirt and khaki pants. He smelled as if he had been drinking. The guy in the booth next to us leaned over sloppily and slapped my customer on the back.

'All right! You got one!' His lips pulled to one side when he spoke, as though someone had reached out and grabbed him by the mouth with a cane.

'Sooo. A bachelor party... looks like the party started before you got here,' I said, making small talk before the song started.

He let out a loud laugh, and his elbows pounded onto the table in front of him. His face landed in the cusp of his hands. 'Yeah. And I think you know the groom. He wants a dance when I'm done.'

'Oh, really? Which one is he?' I asked while unhooking my bra.

He flung his entire arm around in a broad stroke and pointed to a man sitting on a stool outside the booth. 'Right there, in the white shirt.'

As if on cue, the man turned to face me. Unlike his inebriated friends, he seemed in control of his faculties. He sat still and rigid in his seat. His spine was a straight rod, from his lumbar area to the base of his neck. He was looking directly at me. Just as I was getting ready to drop my bra to the floor, I realized who he was. It was my psychology teacher, Dr Stevenson.

I gasped and quickly dropped to the floor of the booth. Dr Stevenson's friend was still watching me, with his face squished and distorted between the palms of his hands. 'Hey there,' he said, twitching his eyebrows like Groucho Marx when I came up to his eye-level. He didn't seem to notice that I had stopped focusing on entertaining him.

I had to be sure it was him. 'Your friend over there, what's his name?'

'Michael. And he wants a dance after this.' He stared at my pelvis as though he was waiting for it to do something.

Michael. Dr Michael Stevenson. It all sank in.

'It's not like you have to put it on your résumé... By the way, which club are you planning on working at?' I remembered his words. His last question had always struck me as odd. What did it matter what club I planned to work at?

I no longer naively believed that all guys who went to strip clubs were ugly, perverted and socially awkward: the ones who could never get girls to like them. I discovered that everyone, from 16-year-old boys with fake IDs, to business-savvy men on lunch breaks, to handsome world travelers in Armani suits patronized the place. But I had always maintained the hope that there were a few woman-loving, self-respecting men out there who would never set foot in a strip club. As Dr Stevenson tumbled from that high place of admiration in my heart, I realized that I was wrong.

'You can go ahead and tell your friend, "No, thanks,"' I said sharply, wishing the song would end so I could put my clothes back on.

'Huh?' the drunk guy looked up at my face.

'I said, you can tell your friend that I won't be doing a table dance for him.' My voice was a little louder than I meant for it to be. I looked up, hoping that Dr Stevenson had heard me. He sat watching his soda swirl in the glass as he stirred it. Dr Stevenson may not have heard me, but his friend in the next booth did.

'What'd she say?' he asked, leaning back over to the guy I was dancing for.

'She said she won't dance for Mike,' he reiterated.

'Come on! He's getting married!' the friend petitioned me with pleading eyes.

I wondered if they knew I used to be one of his students. Were they in on it? I had to know.

'He's a psych teacher, right?' I asked, standing with my hand on my hip.

They shot a glance at each other and looked back at me.

'Yeah,' they said in unison.

I paused and surveyed their questioning faces.

'Well, I'm not dancing for him,' I said firmly, holding my ground.

They dropped the subject and resumed watching Lacey and me for the rest of the song. When it was over, the drunk guy asked for another dance. Lacey's customer darted out of the booth and came back dragging a bashful Dr Stevenson into the seat at Lacey's feet. I stood there waiting for him to look up at me. There was so much I wanted to say to him.

I trusted you. I respected you. You are part of the reason I am in this place! Can you see me? Can you freaking see me? You of all people! You are supposed to be a psychologist. You're supposed to have some insight into people. You were supposed to tell me 'No!' That I am worth more than this, than $14. That I have a bright future in front of me. Didn't you know that coming here tonight would devastate me? That I needed to believe in someone! I needed to believe in you!

I looked directly into his swimming-pool blue eyes and tried to tell him this, but I couldn't speak. Instead, I kept dancing for Dr Stevenson's friend. Dr Stevenson sat motionless and rigid as Lacey danced for him. As soon as the song was over, he tossed a $20 on the table, looked up at me with shame-filled eyes and skirted out of the club.

If there were such a thing as people who lived in buttercup-yellow houses with bright white picket fences and emerald green grass, I thought that Dr Stevenson was one of them. He was my only hope that, somewhere in this world, there was a chance at some sort of normalcy. There was a part of me that wanted to fight for it. I wanted to throw my body in front of the wrecking ball headed straight for that buttercup house in my mind. I wanted to be a woman of integrity and resolve. I wanted to march directly to the dressing room, pack up my things and refuse to take my clothes off for anyone ever again. I wanted to show the world that I could build my own buttercup house one day.

Under the heavy weight of my broken hopes, I watched Dr Stevenson walk out of the door, zipped up my wallet and walked over to the first man I saw.

'Would you like a table dance?'

Twenty

I drove home from school in my Nissan 240 SX. I splurged on the car with the full support and encouragement of Derrick, who preferred to have the Honda to himself anyway. Besides, I was tired of relying on Evan for rides, and it gave me a reason to ignore his excessive phone calls. The car was the nicest and most expensive thing I had ever owned, and I felt good driving it.

When I pulled into the parking lot of our West Los Angeles apartment, I noticed that Derrick's car was gone. I assumed he was playing basketball at the park later than usual. Where else would he be? Stomach growling from a full day of classes and no food, I made a beeline for the apartment, where I plopped down on the couch with a bowl of watermelon. Wanting to lose weight, I had been watching my calories and fat intake very closely since I started stripping. Most days, all I ate was fruit and crackers, or non-fat frozen yogurt. If I was craving gummy bears, I would save up my appetite and grab a small bag of them from the gas station on the way to work, for dinner. Apart from the light-headedness and rumbling belly, my plan was working well. I had easily dropped 15 pounds and was feeling more confident. Even Derrick noticed the difference and, for the first time since high school, he told me I looked good.

After I finished my watermelon, I decided I would get together a load of laundry. There was always a steady stream of dirty whites in need of washing. I never really understood why, but Derrick bought his shoes a size too big and wore two or three pairs of socks to fill them out. Not to mention that he changed into a fresh bunch of socks after basketball each day. That left me with mounds of sweaty socks to pull apart and wash.

Opening the door to Derrick's room, I thought of how unfair

our current set-up was. 'We're just room-mates,' Derrick would tell everyone. When Terrance and Gina came over to visit one day, I inadvertently referred to the bedroom as '*our* bedroom', which contradicted the whole room-mate thing. Terrance and Gina became skeptical about the nature of our relationship.

'Who cares what they think?' I argued, when Derrick became angry with me for the faux pas.

Apparently *he* cared. To prove his point, he decided that we would no longer share a room. 'Fine… I'll sleep on the couch, then,' I said, calling his bluff. Only he wasn't bluffing. Months later, I was still sleeping on the couch, while he sprawled out on the king-size bed with the bedroom to himself.

Just room-mates! I'd like a room-mate to do my laundry and pay my rent and car note, I thought, as I walked over to the closet where he kept his dirty laundry. Such was the nature of our relationship. Bit by bit, Derrick would take what little scraps of a relationship we had away. He gave less and less. Hungry for connection, I gave more and more. Still, I relished what bitter morsels he threw my way. Sleeping on the couch in the same apartment as him was better than not living with him at all.

Just when I thought it couldn't get any worse, I opened the closet to see the last thing on earth a woman would ever expect to see in her closet: *another woman's clothing*. There, neatly hanging in the right section of our closet, in a section all its own, were dresses, shirts, and skirts that did not belong to me.

I frantically yanked the hangers one by one, inspecting the clothing. There had to be a reasonable explanation for this, I thought; there *had* to be. Just then, I heard the front door open and marched into the living room looking for answers. Derrick sat on the couch and placed his hands over the bill of his plain black baseball cap.

'We need to talk.' He never 'needed' to talk. There was a

heaviness in his voice that caused my rage to halt instantly. A deep fear rose in me. I had a sense that something dreadful was about to happen. My entire body began to shake, and I sank to the floor on the other side of the coffee table.

'What is it?' My words were a shaky whisper.

'Gina's pregnant,' he said, tugging at the bill of his hat, covering his face.

'So what?' It had to be Terrance's, right? Please, please let it be Terrance's, I pleaded on the inside.

'She says it's mine.' He still wouldn't look me in the eye.

'But… but I thought you said you never had sex with her. You told me you never had sex with her…You lied to me,' I said, through sudden heavy sobs. It was naive of me to have ever believed it. Did I ever *really* believe it? I wondered.

'We only had sex once,' he tried to reason with me.

I felt a hard black ball develop in the center of my chest. I held my tears tightly and looked up at him. He really expected me to believe that. He really thought I was that dumb.

'Her mom kicked her out of the house.' There was a long moment of silence. I could hear my own heart pounding heavily. 'She's going to stay here for a while.'

'The clothing! That's why there's women's clothing in the closet? She already moved in? You didn't even think about asking me first?' I said, trying to make sense of it all.

'What was I supposed to do? She has nowhere else to go. I didn't want her out on the streets,' he explained.

Oh, great. Now I am supposed to feel sorry for the girl he got pregnant, I thought.

'It'll only be for a little while,' he tried to console me.

'Then what? It wasn't supposed to be this way!' I had always hoped that he would get over his fear of commitment and we would start a family together. That simple hope was what I had been sacrificing for. That hope is what I had been *selling* myself for.

'I don't know.' There was an unfamiliar, yet genuine sincerity in his voice. He didn't know. He had no idea. 'Maybe I'll get custody. Maybe you and I can raise the child.'

'Is that supposed to make me feel better? You expect me to believe that she is going to let some other woman raise her child?' There was a part of me that wished it were true. That she would just go away for good and leave him and me to take care of it. Then it could go back to being just the two of us. He stood up and started walking to the door.

'She's waiting downstairs in the car. I told her that I was going to come up and talk to you first. I'm gonna go down and get her now.' He said it slowly, as if he was talking to a mad woman on the verge of a breakdown. I suppose I was mad to endure all of this.

I couldn't bear to watch her walk in my door, so I locked myself in the bathroom. I listened as the front door opened and closed. Then the bedroom door opened... and closed. I turned the faucet on so they couldn't hear me cry. My life was not my own. This had to be somebody else's life. Oh, God – if there is a God – please help me! Please help me, I pleaded.

For all I cared, the man I was dancing for was just another nameless, faceless, ageless man with cash in his pocket. On autopilot, I went through the usual repertoire of movements I had come to refer to as dance. *Sway, sway, sway, bra off; sway, sway, bend, panties down*; and so on.

The man sitting at eye level with my pelvis was eagerly leaning forward to get a better view. As I moved in closer, he jet his neck out and thrust his chin forward as if to try to reach me. I recoiled instantly and issued my usual warning. 'No touching!'

I said firmly, holding up a finger to his face to emphasize my point. Through thick, smudgy glasses, the man glanced over into the booth next to us, where a busty colleague of mine pressed a man's face into her bosom.

'I don't care what she's doing. There's no touching allowed,' I reiterated.

I was one of a few girls in the club who actually adhered to the 'no touching' rule, not out of a sense of obligation to the law, but out of repulsion at being touched. Even when it came to Derrick, outside of sex we never touched. Although I complained that I wanted more affection, deep down I felt safer in a relationship void of intimacy. Every muscle in my body tensed when people touched me. When I said 'no touching', I meant it.

Surely this mousy, half-balding, beady-eyed man would heed my warning.

I continued dancing routinely, paying little attention to the man or the dance I was doing for him. Instead, as I waved my pelvis in front of his face I watched Porsche on stage, with her pony-like gait. She flung her feet out from the knee with each step. The thigh-high patent-leather boots she wore exaggerated her silly little walk.

As I was analyzing the quirkiness of Porsche's walk, I suddenly felt something warm and slimy against my skin. The man licked me! I leapt to the back of the booth, as far from him as possible. For a moment my body was still and paralyzed. Then I remembered the words of an off-duty cop who frequented the club. 'If someone assaults you, you have a ten-second reaction time. In ten seconds, you can do whatever you want without consequence.' He told me this after I recounted a story in which a man had grabbed at me despite my 'no touching' warnings.

Ten seconds; I have ten seconds, my mind raced. Rage

At age six, playing with my baby brother, Noah.

This photo (right) was taken during a modeling shoot when I was 14, just prior to being kicked out of Jr. High.

Dancing in the backyard of our childhood home.

The house in Venice where I spent most of my childhood.

In the alley behind my house, aged 15. As a result of sexual abuse and rape, my identity had became heavily intertwined with my sexuality.

Working at the early childhood education program. Soon after this photo was taken, I quit to pick up more shifts at the strip club.

The night I tried out my new persona, "Monique", on the Los Angeles nightlife (age 20).

Years later…
having become a Christian.

Meeting Tanya in ballet class changed the trajectory of my life forever – it was she who led me to the Lord. Here we are in hysterics at a friend's wedding reception – we're known for laughing fitfully over the silliest nonsense.

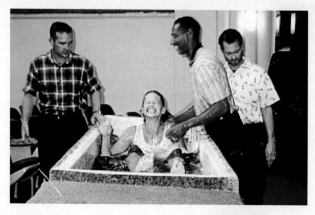

On the day of my baptism with Pastor Philip Wagner (far right). More than a religious ceremony, this signified the great healing and transformation that had taken place in my life.

I began studying psychology in an attempt to understand my chaotic life. I'm pictured here with my proud mother and brother on the day of my graduation from UCLA in 2000. Three years later, I went back to do a Masters in Social Welfare.

My Grandma Mary and Auntie Krissi looking regal at my graduation celebration brunch.

My beautiful daughter, Johnny Ella. I intend to raise her so that she knows full well she is loved beyond measure, and a daughter of *the* King.

God never wastes a hurt: In 2003, a vision was birthed from my broken past when I founded Treasures – an effort to reach women in the sex industry with the message that they are loved, valued and purposed. Pictured here is the Treasures Leadership Team during our annual retreat.

Volunteer, Sarah M. during an outreach in Vegas. The last time she was there she was still working in the industry. On this trip, she could hold her head high as she reached out to those who were still there.

The Treasures Volunteer Team at our Annual 2013 Dinner for a Treasure Fundraising Gala.

2013 Gala, standing amongst brave 'liberators', sharing their stories of freedom.

With other volunteers at a porn convention in Los Angeles.

In August 2009, the strip club I used to work at was closed. The building was leveled and turned into an airport parking lot.

With friends Jennifer Smith, Pastor Holly Wagner and Ashley Abercrombie celebrating the 25th Anniversary of Oasis – the church I call 'home'.

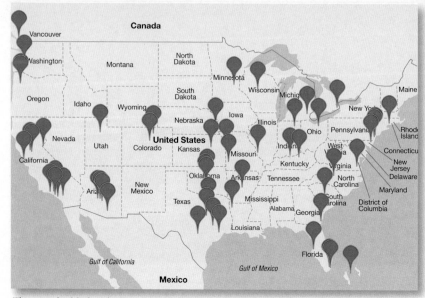

This map highlights the Treasures-Trained outreaches in the US and Canada. As of 2013, we have trained sex industry outreach leaders in 70 cities on four continents. Our goal is to see flourishing outreaches developed in every major city on the planet.

On the set of *Sex Rehab* with Dr. Drew (2009). I was invited on the show to share my story with other women working to overcome issues of sexual brokenness. Since the inception of Treasures, I have had the privilege to be featured in various media outlets including *The Tyra Banks Show* and *Glamour* magazine.

swelled inside me: rage against him and Derrick and Gina and the customer in the booth next to us and my professor and Maurice. All the rage I had ever had and stuffed deep down in my gut rose up.

Ten. I smacked him clear across the face with all the force I could muster. His glasses flew off into the next booth as he sat there stunned. *Nine.* I punched him in the side of the head. *Eight.* I plucked the stiletto off my foot and began beating him with the thick platform. *Seven. Six. Five. Four.* With my bare foot I kicked him in the chest, which sent him stumbling off the stool. He landed on his back with his knees bent up, like a baby waiting for a diaper change. *Three.* I jumped out of the booth, kicked him in the ribs and stomped on his chest.

'Monique! Hey-hey-hey! Monique!' The security had just noticed that I was beating this man.

Two. One. I counted to myself, breathing heavily; panting, shaking, wanting to finish the job.

The security pulled the man up off the floor; I hollered, 'He licked me! That man licked me and I told him there was no touching!'

The security grabbed the man by the jacket and began yanking him away from the booths.

'He better pay me first!' I demanded. My colleague and her customer had stopped to watch the scene unfold. Her customer handed him his glasses. One of the lenses had popped out of the frame.

'All right, pay up.' The security backed me. Shakily, the man pulled a $20 bill out of his wallet, handed it to me and paused. Don't tell me this man was waiting for his change!

'Goodbye!' I said, wearing a sarcastic smile and shooing him along with my hands.

The police showed up at the club half an hour later and

called me into the back premises for questioning. I was surprised the guy had the guts to call them when *he* had been the one to assault me. I was the victim... wasn't I?

There were two officers, standing stiff in their uniforms, stuffed with bulletproof vests. One of them, a tall lanky man with slick black hair, asked me questions and took notes on a little pad of paper. The other, short and stout, stood to the side and observed.

'So what seems to be the problem here? The man outside says that you attacked him,' the taller cop asked me.

Standing there in six-inch heels, a bra and panties, I stated my case. 'That man licked me! He is the one who assaulted *me*! And if I am not mistaken, I am allowed a ten-second reaction time... I told him that there was no touching allowed and he *licked* me! If anyone should be calling the cops, it should be me!'

Maybe it was the heels, or the fact that I was half-naked and working in a strip club, but somehow my statement did not evoke empathy or compassion from the officers. They looked at me with dull eyes and stoic expressions.

'Listen. I think you need to apologize to the guy,' the cop advised.

'What? Are you listening to me? The guy *licked* me! And you want me to apologize to him!?'

'He is thinking of filing battery charges against you,' he continued, his tone bland and monotonous.

'He can't do that! I only attacked him because he assaulted me. And I have ten seconds reaction time... right?' I began to second-guess the off-duty cop's advice.

'At best, this will turn into a mutual battery. He will file charges against you, and you would file against him. I think if you just apologize to him, he'll drop it,' the cop explained.

Battery charges. How's that for a résumé, I thought to

myself. As much as I loathed doing it, pride was not worth going to jail for. Dignity, on the other hand, was worth fighting for; only I didn't feel I had much left. The shorter cop retrieved the assaulted victim of a man from whatever hole he had been hiding in during my interview. With puny little shuffling steps, standing inches behind the protection of the officer, the man showed up to receive his apology.

You horrible, disgusting, wimpy man! You should be apologizing to me! I screamed inside my head. I wanted to say it out loud and to beat him all over again. This time I wanted to break more than his glasses. Instead, I folded my arms, caulked my hips to one side and looked up at the ceiling in the most defiant, unapologetic stance I could muster.

'I'm sorry.' My voice was seething with anger and untruth. I was *not* sorry. But those stupid little meaningless words were going to keep me from going to 52 weeks of anger management classes and spending a night in jail. Hands in his pockets, squirming, the man nodded his head vigorously, accepting my tainted offering of peace.

Anger coursed though the blood in my veins as I stomped off to the dressing room. My colleagues were waiting there with empathy and curiosity.

'What happened? What did that guy do? Why were the police here?' they wanted to know.

Of course, the very nature of the business had each of us pit against the other out on the floor, striving to make the most money, striving to shine the brightest. But in the locker room, we were all the same. We were girls. And most of us had something in common: we pretty much didn't like men. Sure, there was Grace who loved everyone and told us that she saw beauty in every man who walked in the club; I had a hard time believing her. And there was Chelsea, who said that she actually liked stripping because it was the first time in her life that she had got attention from men. But for the rest of us, the locker room was a place where we could vent about the jerk who didn't tip us, or the one who looked down on us like he couldn't be bothered with us approaching him for a dance. 'Like he could do better! If you can do better than me, then why are you in a freaking strip club?' we would lament.

And so I poured out my heart and my story to this room of women. Who else would truly understand? Who else knew what it felt like to endure the loathsome, unwanted gaze of a stranger over our naked bodies for a small sum of money? To feel obligated to smile and act as though you would like nothing more in this world than his leering eyes piercing through you. And then to have the stringy little boundaries you set up to maintain some ounce of dignity crossed and disregarded entirely! Who else could know what that felt like?

Lexi sat down beside me and put her arm around my shoulders. Packaged inside her petite 90-pound frame was a vivacious and feisty personality. Her smile was large and bright, her singing voice larger and brighter still. When she sang she invoked the power of Etta James, and Aretha Franklin, and the velvet elegance of Billie Holiday.

'Monique... You need a night out. What are you doing for Halloween? We should go out and have some fun!' she suggested.

I took her up on her offer and gave up trying not to fit in at the club; trying to distinguish myself from the other girls. I moved out of the tiny locker room on the outskirts of the club and found my place in the large and bustling center of it all.

Later that week, Lexi, Jade, and I hit the night clubs in Hollywood for Halloween. Lexi and I dressed up as big cats. She was a tiger and I was a leopard. I paraded down Sunset in a leopard print G-string leotard and stilettos. Jade was a mouse. More specifically, *my* mouse. She wore a collar around her neck and I held the leash.

Until that point, 'Monique' stayed in the strip club. I didn't think that there was a place for her in the real world. 'Harmony' walked around in the light of day, hiding any traces of attractiveness behind baggy sweats, glasses and ponytails. But that night, it was 'Monique' who ate sushi for the first time in some Hollywood hipster restaurant, before hopping to the front of the winding lines at a string of nightclubs on Sunset Boulevard. And it was the scantily clad 'Monique' and her comrades who turned the heads of men who couldn't buy us or pay to see us naked if they wanted to, because we were not for sale. Not that night.

Sex and sexuality permeated everything Monique did. It colored all her interactions, until she didn't know any other way to interact. So it was 'Monique' who, knowing no other way to build an intimate friendship with another human, slept with Lexi, after drinking so much alcohol in one hour that she had to be escorted out of the club for inadvertently slugging an unsuspecting waitress.

But it was 'Harmony' who suffered from the hangover. My head hurt so horribly that wearing sunglasses inside my own apartment did little to stop the throbbing. For the next three days, I puked until black bile was spilling out of my mouth and into the toilet and onto my chest and car and bed and any other place or thing I happened to be near.

The worst hangover in hangover history was not enough to keep 'Monique' from trying to carve an identity for herself outside the strip club. Two weeks later we met at Jade's apartment, where I changed into skin-tight black pants, stiletto heels and a black bustier. Lexi wore a sheer black shirt that completely exposed her $10,000 enhancement. Her boyfriend Marcel, a brown-skinned, smooth-shaven man with a polished pompadour, came with her. Before he whisked her away to Tinsel Town, she met him in Hawaii, where he allegedly gave up his career as a pimp to manage his and Lexi's singing careers. His own singing voice was as slick and as high as his hair – both matching those of his idol, Jackie Wilson. He and Lexi had all the talent they needed to become stars. Until then, Lexi continued to support him with the money she made at the strip club.

With her professional MAC brushes and a box of make-up the size of a carry-on suitcase, Lexi did my hair and make-up, crooning the entire time about how I should wear it more often. 'You're so beautiful, Harmony,' she said in a soft, seductive voice as Marcel looked on from a distance. The faint smell of cigarettes on her breath was hidden behind toothpaste and chewing gum. Hearing her speak my real name made me shudder slightly. 'Harmony' didn't know how to respond to the flirtatious advances of a woman, and 'Monique' wasn't drunk enough to jump in. When Lexi finished painting my face, I looked at myself in Lotus's black-lacquered vanity. I hardly recognized myself. Staring back at me was a smoky-eyed vixen.

Apart from the lack of shirts, the night was like many others I had spent getting ready to go to a club with my friends in high school; that is, until Sierra showed up with her man-friend. Sierra had shiny blonde hair, knowing eyes, and a figure that matched her name entirely. Everything about her was golden and curvy. At the club, there was elitism about her. She seldom came to work, and when she did, she seemed to have pre-arranged appointments with wealthy clientele: men donning thick gold chains and sparkling diamond rings.

'What are you doing here, Monique?' she said, pulling me to the side minutes after arriving.

I drew my head back in defense and looked at her, confused. 'Why wouldn't I be here?'

'I'm sorry, honey. You don't belong here. You shouldn't be hanging out with these girls...' she whispered.

I wanted to be angry at her. I wanted to be offended. But beyond her words, I heard genuine concern in her voice that was almost motherly. Still, my pride wanted to show her that at the ripe age of 20, I had seen it all, done it all, and I could handle it all.

To make my point, when Sierra's man-friend pulled vials of cocaine from the inside pocket of his designer jacket and they all started doing lines, I didn't flinch. I wanted to grab Lexi by the hair, take her in my arms, and tell her that coke ruins relationships: it destroys families and devastates lives. Instead, I kept my mouth shut, and casually sprawled out on Lotus's leopard print bedspread, feigning apathy. And when Lexi and her boyfriend Marcel came and lay beside me, I stayed as still and natural as possible.

'She's sexy...' Sierra's man-friend commented to Marcel, as if Lexi were not a living breathing human being with ears that could hear him; as if she was a picture in a magazine or a mannequin in a window. Still Lexi smiled a scripted smile. It was how a non-woman was supposed to respond.

'You want some?' Marcel said, pointing to Lexi.

My eyes flashed to Lexi, whose smile was at half-mast; just enough so that this man who was looking at her didn't know the difference. Marcel had offered her up to a stranger as if she was his to offer. The air was heavy around me, and I hoped that someone would break through it with a wild and boisterous laugh, indicating that it was all an ill-humored joke. The laugh never came. And right before my eyes, in a brightly lit bedroom filled with a half-dozen acquaintances and strangers, Marcel gave away his girlfriend to another man.

But for the dim light seeping out of the bedroom, the house was dark when I got home from work. I had hoped that Derrick and Gina would be sleeping by now. It was easier for me to fall asleep when I wasn't bothered by the persistence of my compulsion to play detective. For the rest of the night, I would strain to hear their muffled voices behind the closed door of the bedroom.

I tiptoed over to the large, walk-in storage closet directly across from the bedroom and pulled out the brown leather-bound Bible my grandmother had sent me. It had been a gift to her from my Auntie Krissy, but for some reason my grandmother shipped it off to me. It was a great place to hide money, because it was the last place in the house that Derrick would look in.

When I first took the job stripping, I had planned to save some cash and pay down my debts, but holding on to money was near impossible with Derrick around. I knew the only way I would ever be able to save anything would be to hide it. This is where the Bible came in handy. Each night, I placed a crisp $100 bill into its pages. As the stash grew, the Bible widened. When the Bible became suspiciously plump, I knew I had to move it. A savings account would leave a paper trail, so I opened up a safety deposit box to stash my savings.

Of course, there was more to it than just hiding money. I also had to lie to Derrick about how much money I made each night. More than weigh on my conscience, this nagged at my pride. In a business where I was my own commodity, the amount of money I brought home was, in a sense, a reflection of how much I was worth. So telling Derrick that I made $500 instead of $600, or $800 instead of $1,000, meant cheapening myself. If

I had a really slow night, I wouldn't even put aside money, for the simple fact that I couldn't bring myself to tell him that I had only made $200.

Standing in the closet, I flipped open the Bible, and my eyes landed on the faint scribble of my grandmother's handwriting. I was surprised to see that she had even dared to write in a book she considered so holy. As I pulled it closer for examination, her writing and her heart became clear. In pencil was one simple word, written next to a gently underlined passage: 'Harmony'.

Beside my name was the Scripture 'Blessed are the poor in spirit, for they shall inherit the Kingdom...'

I used my thumb to hold the page, and quickly flipped through the rest of the Bible to see if there was any other place where my grandmother had dared to write inside her cherished text. Nothing. I pictured my grandmother, sitting in her bed reading her Bible under the light of her antique lamp, reading faithfully and coming across that sentence. 'Blessed are the poor in spirit for they shall inherit the Kingdom'. She must have taken comfort in the idea that, somehow, her 'poor' grandchild could or would some day be blessed. Imagining her searching for a pencil in the cabinet of her nightstand and carefully writing my name in her Holy Book softened my heart towards her, and what I always thought were her religious rantings about going to church and reading the Bible.

'Harmny.' The syllables of my name ran together in her East Texas accent. 'You really need to go to church. And you should read your Bible every day, too!'

Why? Why would I go to church or read my Bible? Just so she could sleep at night knowing her big, angry God wouldn't send me to hell if I played by some man-made rules? I wanted to argue with her, but it was pointless. But standing there in my closet, holding her prized Bible in my hands, I realized that there was something caring and personal at the heart of her 'ranting' that I had never seen before.

She wanted her grandbaby to be blessed.

I sat on the pull-out sofa and examined a small trickle of blood running down my foot. Each night, the straps of my stilettos pushed and rubbed and sliced their way deeper into the thin flesh of my ankles, leaving me with matching gashes on each side. I doused the cuts with peroxide, and covered them with a salve of comfrey and goldenseal. They would not heal, because each time a scab began to form, I danced again. Surely this will scar, I thought to myself. If I am ever able to leave this life behind me, I will bear the evidence of it still.

I turned out all the lights and slipped beneath my scratchy, mismatched sheets. In the next room I could hear the hushed sounds of laughter, and I could feel my heart as it cracked and spilled inside my chest. Then quiet filled the room, like a stiff, black blanket. The silence hurt even more than the laughter, and my heart ached as I envisioned her lying in his arms.

The bedroom door opened, and I watched through feigned sleep as Gina walked into the living room. She was wearing his green button-down shirt, no pants, and a pair of his white, oversized socks. They were the ones I bought in packs of five at the swap meet. She pranced right through the room, strutting in his clothes like a peacock. She *wanted* me to see her.

I could hear her in my kitchen, helping herself to my soda. *Get out of my house!* I screamed in my head. On her way back to the bedroom, I noticed that she had not one glass, but two. She was bringing him something to drink. That was my job. I was supposed to be the one bringing him soda late at night. I wanted to tear her hair out and throw the soda on her face.

When she went back to the room, I turned on the lights,

pulled out a textbook and tried to lose myself in my studies: *Psychology: The Study of the Human Mind*. If I could only make sense of my own! My very existence in this place neared insanity. I kept reading the same sentence about classical versus operant conditioning again and again, until I finally gave up and headed for the restroom, where I dulled the pain with the only thing that ever worked: more pain.

I pulled out a pair of tweezers from my medicine cabinet, and sat on the closed lid of the toilet. With quick, methodical, tiny yanking motions, one by one, I plucked out my pubic hairs, sure to maintain a perfect triangle. The surrounding area was already smooth and clean from constant and obsessive upkeep, but I pulled and picked at any and all hairs that even dared to protrude from the surface of my skin. When there was no more hair left to pluck, I pressed the tweezers down around any faint spots of pre-budded hairs to see if I could manage to rip them out. I did this until my neck muscles hurt from firmly pressing my chin to my chest for better viewing. My delicate skin was red and welted.

I went back to bed, a dull throbbing pain permeating my groin. Just as rest had permanently eluded me, sleep would not come to me either. I tried changing positions, and mindsets, and anything I could think of. I contemplated driving to the 24-hour Home Depot, where I often found comfort in walking up and down aisles of hardware, and paint, and tools, and everything a person would need to build, fix, and maintain a home. Rubbernecked men with sun-browned skin and paint-splattered overalls stared at me unapologetically, as if they had never seen a woman in a hardware store. And I imagine that few women indeed did show up at 4.00 am, wander aimlessly, and leave without a purchase. Still, I found a strange comfort in the vastness of it all. At Home Depot, very little made sense to me, but it all had a place and a purpose and *someone* knew what it all meant. That was enough to help me sleep at night, most nights. But not this night.

The agony of staying there on the pull-out couch was less than the agony of walking out and surrendering my home to another woman. So I stayed. And listened, and waited, and hoped that one day, by the sheer strength of my resolve *not* to leave, it would be me bringing him soda in the night once again.

MaSyh and I had always been close. We'd been friends since we were two, and had been raised almost like sisters. I knew I should never have allowed her to come and stay with me. But I was never one to say 'no' to her, and she was never one to listen anyway.

'Are you sure you want to come stay here? I don't have an extra bed or anything. Why don't you stay with Auntie Nishtay, and I will come visit you?' I tried to convince her.

'Harmony, now why wouldn't I just come stay with you for a couple of days? Plus I am going to be spending most of the summer with Auntie, anyway.'

'Well, the pull-out couch isn't that big. And it's not that comfortable,' I noted.

'You mean to tell me that you don't even sleep in your own bed? What the hell is going on over there?'

'MaSyh, it's a long story. Derrick has the bedroom now because I had the bedroom at the last place. Plus I sleep in there sometimes, too.' I tried to rationalize an insane arrangement.

'That don't make no kinda sense! You sleeping on the couch in your own damn house. *Any*way, I'm still coming.' And so she did.

I hoped that MaSyh would show up and that, for nostalgia's sake, we could all go back to laughing and goofing off, as we did when she, Derrick, and I spent the summers at the pool. But too much had changed since then. I wasn't really allowed to goof off any more. I was a woman, and according to Derrick women were supposed to be silent and sexy. Seen and not heard. He had always told me that everything would be just fine, if I could learn to keep my mouth shut. I was better at sexy than silent. No matter how hard I tried, my jaws flapped and his temper snapped, over and over again. And of course, it was always my fault. And Derrick had long since given up on laughing. On the rare occasions when he did, it always felt timed and calculated, controlled and intentional, the way a chess player moves a pawn.

I could only hope – no, *pray* – that Gina would miraculously move back in with her mother before MaSyh arrived. No such luck. When MaSyh showed up, Derrick wasn't home. He was at the park, playing pick-up basketball, as was his routine for at least four hours of the day. Gina must have been with him, because she was gone too. For once, I was grateful for his hobby, because it put off what I was sure would be a drama-filled encounter with MaSyh.

'Let's go get something to eat.' I suggested this casually, but inside I was pleading.

'Where's Derrick?' MaSyh prodded. She still didn't know about Gina.

'Oh, he's not going to be home until later.'

'Didn't he know I was coming?' She seemed offended that he hadn't arranged his day around her arrival. The Derrick she knew when we were kids – the one with wavy brown hair, long gangly limbs, and barely enough armpit hair to make up Hitler's mustache – would have. But the new Derrick didn't make a habit of accommodating anybody.

'Yeah, but he plays basketball in the day.' *Please let it go*, I silently pleaded.

'He couldn't miss one day of basketball, knowing that I am almost never in LA any more?' she complained. I knew it was going to be a long weekend. She hadn't even seen Derrick yet, and she was already offended.

When we got home from Campos Tacos, Derrick was in the bedroom with the door closed. I could hear the sound of grunt-filled jabs and high-flying kicks, as he played Street Fighter video games. I hoped with all the hope I could muster that Gina wasn't inside that room with him. Then I heard her cackling laugh as she cheered Derrick on.

'Derrick's home?' MaSyh asked, and, as if on cue, the door opened and he emerged, lanky and tall, still wearing his sweaty basketball shorts and jersey. He glanced at MaSyh, and then at me, continuing his bee-line for the kitchen.

'What's up?' he said, without looking back at either of us, or waiting for a response. After pouring soda into a large, blue plastic cup, he went right back to the bedroom.

'Peace out,' he said as he closed the door.

MaSyh's eyes were wild with fury, her body tense and still; like a cobra waiting to strike. I knew this stance well, and drew back instinctively.

'He done lost his mind,' she said slowly, still taking in the shock of it. 'He didn't even come talk to me.'

'MaSyh, please don't. Just please…' I begged.

Her eyes darted to mine, and whether it was out of kindness or pity, my pleading kept her at bay.

For the rest of the night, I tried to do the girly chat, catch-me-up-on-all-the-details-of-your-life thing, but it was useless. My senses were heightened, and adrenaline was pumping through my body, as if someone were bound to toss a grenade through the window of my apartment. Besides, I couldn't tell her much about my life that was true, other than the fact that I was still going to school and studying psychology. There were too many things I was ashamed of.

The rest of the evening, I did my best to avoid telling the truth with as few lies as possible. I just couldn't bring myself to say: 'Oh yes, since you've been gone, I have taken up stripping. I bend over naked in men's faces for a living. And the girl in the room is Derrick's latest conquest. The good news is, I think he finally stopped seeing that 17-year-old high-school girl who lives in Chattsworth. The bad news is, Gina is carrying his child, and it looks like I will be the one buying diapers. How about you? What have you been up to?'

Throughout the night, MaSyh watched the bedroom door, and I imagined she was thinking much the same thing that I was. *When is that girl going to leave?*

She didn't leave. Eventually, Derrick and Gina turned the television off in the bedroom, and the house was filled with the loudest silence I have ever heard. MaSyh and I sat on the couch in a stalemate.

'Well, I guess we should hit the sack.' My voice cut through the space between us.

MaSyh stared blankly at the dull white walls of my apartment and nodded her head, as if in a state of shock. I stood up, began dragging sheets and pillows from the hall closet, and proceeded to make a place for us on the rickety old pull-out couch that had belonged to Derrick's mother before the stroke.

That night, neither of us slept. MaSyh tossed fitfully. Each time she moved, the pull-out bounced revengefully, jabbing me with its failing mattress springs and poky iron frame. And every so often, throughout the long night, MaSyh would find words for her anguish.

'That boy is sleeping in the bed with her, knowing full well we are out here on this couch. And you're letting him.'

Silence.

'Harmony!' She sprang up and looked at me. 'What the hell is wrong with you? Seriously! I think that you have really lost it!'

Silence.

'This is B*ll S**t! It really is.'

Silence.

'This is madness! Am I the only sane person in this damn house?'

Silence. And then, a solution…

'I know exactly what I am going to do…'

Her tone was enough to make me quit pretending I had been able to sleep through her tirades. I opened my eyes and turned to face her.

'What, MaSyh? What are you going to do?'

'I am calling my brother.' That's all she said. That is all she had to say to send panic through my body. Her cousin was already *in* jail: for murder. Who knows what her brother might do?!

'No!' I whispered, as loudly and authoritatively as I could. 'You can't do that!'

'Why not? *You're* not going to do anything. And I can't just sit here and let this happen. I'm calling him.'

'Please! No! Please don't!' I begged.

'And now you want to protect him? That crazy man has another woman, in *your house*! And you want to protect him? You really have lost your mind!' she raged.

Tears spilled onto my pillow. 'Please don't; please,' was all I had the strength to whimper. Involvement in a conspiracy to murder – that was the last thing I needed. Would he send out some teenagers eager for street cred to do a messy drive-by while Derrick was at the park, playing ball? Or would he do it himself – execution style – straight in the head, with a silencer? I pictured the vulnerable look of surprise that would fall across Derrick's face while staring down the barrel of a gun. My heart sank to the pit of me. And if Derrick died, surely I would have to follow. I couldn't exist without him.

I spent the night hoping there was a God, and praying to him fiercely. And, for what felt like the first time in my life, my prayers were answered. The next morning, MaSyh emerged from the bathroom with the cordless phone in her hand. She had made the call.

'You're lucky his ass is in jail right now. That's all I have to say. 'Cuz if he wasn't…'

She didn't have to finish her sentence. I had stayed up all night, imagining it.

It was a slow Sunday night. The weather had been warm and beautiful, the skies bright indigo. It was the kind of day that men spent on outings with their families, forgoing their evening trip to the strip club. I stood at the back of the club, scanning the half-dozen men peppered through the room. Brandy, a sassy woman with the legs of a ballerina, was the only one doing table dances. She was with one of her regulars. Most of the other girls were in the dressing room, chatting and primping, waiting for things to pick up. I made an agreement with myself: if I made $300 by 10.00 pm, then I could take a 15-minute break to eat a bag of pretzels. Otherwise, I would have to stay on floor, making my rounds and keeping myself visible to potential customers.

A man with slick black hair and deep-set eyes, wearing a black blazer and slacks, walked in and sat at the foot of the stage. Leaning back, with his ankle propped up on his knee, and his arm perched on the back of the chair next to him, he took up more space than he needed.

When Mandy, with her knobby bones and stringy frame,

walked on stage, his eyes bounced around the room looking at everything but her. She wandered to and fro atop her stilettos, stopping in front of each customer at the stage, robotically bending over, or lifting her leg above their head, as a male dog would above a fire hydrant. Occasional hip sways indicated that she was, in fact, dancing. The man in the blazer hardly seemed to notice her. Despite his seeming lack of interest, somewhere towards the middle of her song, he pulled a stack of bills from his inside jacket pocket and flicked a wad of 20 one-dollar bills in the air as she walked by. The money worked like a charm. Her sunken eyes glowed with a dim glow as she ceased her wandering and danced for him alone for the rest of her song.

It was nearing 10.00 pm, so I went to the locker room to count my money and check my progress. Jade was naked and sprawled out on a beach towel on the floor, with a bottle of Jack Daniels in her hand. I stopped to look at her, when Grace, a 40-something-year-old platinum blonde with silicon, ruby-red lips, chimed in.

'She's drunk. She's drinking every night now.'

'Moooownick! Moooownick!' Jade called out as she attempted to pull herself up into a sitting position.

'What's going on, Jade? You been drinking?' I asked, though it was obvious.

'Yeah. That's why I got this beer gut now,' she said, grabbing a handful of flesh from her abdomen. 'The customers don't like fat girls, Mownick,' she said, with her Vietnamese accent. 'That's why I can't make any money around here, lately.'

'You're not making any money because you get drunk every night, Jade,' Grace corrected her.

Grace and I were two of the very few sober girls in the club. After overcoming an addiction to cocaine that she had supported by prostituting herself to the patrons of the club, Grace preached abstinence from mind-altering substances. She had left that life behind – and moved on to more respectable things, like producing her own porn, in which she was the star of every film.

And sobriety wasn't all she preached. Thanks to her Southern Baptist upbringing, she also preached about things like not gossiping in the dressing room, loving the customers because we are supposed to love everybody on this green earth, and forgiving people no matter what they do to you. It was all so airy-fairy. But that was Grace.

'I just don't understand why my best friend won't forgive me,' Grace lamented one day.

'Why is she mad at you?' I asked.

Grace pushed her bright lips into a pout, and slumped her shoulders like a five-year-old. 'I slept with her husband while she was in labor with their child.'

My bottom jaw dropped open. I couldn't even hide my shock.

'You don't understand...' she piped, before I could comment. 'We went to get her suitcase so we could meet her at the hospital. I saw her wedding dress in the closet and thought it would be fun to put it on. We just got caught up in the moment. Me in her wedding dress, her getting ready to have his baby.'

'You have to be kidding me, Grace. You expect her to forgive you after that?'

She responded with a pout and doe eyes that I assume she expected would win me over. That kind of look worked only on men. Grace whisked out of the room for her turn on stage, and I proceeded to count my money: *20, 40, 60, 80...*

'Mownick... Mownick... I need to go jogging.' Jade was still lying on her towel.

'What you *need* to do is lay off all that Jack...' *140, 160, 180...* I counted.

'Mooooownick...'

'Yes, Jade?' I responded, in the most patient voice I could muster.

She lifted her head up to look at me, before letting it drop hard on the floor.

'I can't remember what I was going to say.'

'OK, Jade. Let me know if you remember.' *250... Dang!* I still hadn't made $300, so I headed back to the floor.

When I walked out of the locker room, Grace was on stage, relishing hundreds of one-dollar bills that flittered about her as the man in the blazer tossed them in her direction. I quickly scanned the DJ's board, to see how long it would be before it was my turn on stage. With only three girls before me, I hoped the guy would stick around long enough to see me. *Maybe it won't be such a bad night after all*, I thought.

When Grace's set was finished, she bent over on her hands and knees to collect her treasure. Frantically trying to pick up all the cash before the next girl's song started, she gathered her money and pulled it into a pile against her chest. Apparently Grace was the only one that tickled his fancy, because when the next few girls got on stage, he tossed a mere handful of money at each one. When it was finally my turn, I hoped that he would like *my* performance enough to repeat *his*.

Not wanting to appear desperate, I gave equal time and attention to the men at each point of the stage. My tactic seemed to work, because within a minute, the man in the blazer was casting bundles of ones onto the stage. They flitted and flickered about me like an approving shower. I twirled across the stage with the pouring rain of adoration floating around me. Yes, it was going to be a good night.

I continued to play the game, giving him no more attention than the other men sitting at the stage. This was *my* performance, after all. Each time he thrust a gob of ones towards me, I flashed him a flirtatious smile and continued my show. Bills littered the entire floor. I had to walk carefully, so as not to slip in my six-inch stilettos.

When my set was finished, like Grace I dropped to my knees, and began scraping together piles of money. Just when I had successfully pulled together a small mountain of cash, the man in the blazer threw another fistful at me. I laughed playfully, hoping he would continue. The DJ stalled the next girl's set by making all sorts of announcements about free admission during the day and the price of table dances. The man in the blazer tossed another wad of ones at me.

Then it hit me. This whole scene had nothing to do with me, or how much he liked me. It had nothing to do with how attractive I was, or my acrobatic pole tricks. It was all about him. This man was more entertained by seeing me scurrying and scuttling around the floor chasing after his money than he was by my dancing. This wasn't about him lavishing me with adoration, but about fueling his own pride.

I wanted his money, but playing to his ego made me feel undignified. There had to be an easier way to get the money, without groveling for it. An idea came to me. I got up from the floor and called to one of the bus boys.

'Eduardo, would you mind bringing me a broom and a garbage bag, please?' I asked.

Within seconds, Eduardo appeared from behind the curtain with the requested items. I began sweeping the bills into a great big pile in the middle of the stage, and Eduardo helped me stuff them in the garbage bag. I looked up to see the man in the blazer watching us dump his money into the large black trash bag, and there was a little less glimmer in his eyes; a little less pride. The garbage bag served a greater purpose than practicality. I was sweeping this man's ego up into that trash bag, and it felt good.

I tossed the sack of money over my back and took it to the locker room to count my booty. Grace was sitting on the floor in the corner of the room, feasting on a buffet of candy and chips she had bought from the liquor store on her way to work.

'Wow! He liked you,' Grace said, in a small, childish voice. It was the same voice she used with the customers when she was trying to coax them into staying for another table dance.

'Well, he seemed to like you too, Grace,' I said, trying to reassure her.

Competition was innate to the business. Grace and I were two of the top earners in the club, which meant we were quietly comparing ourselves with each other. We were completely different. Twenty years my senior, with straightened, bleachy hair, she was always in full make-up and adorned with fake diamonds. She cascaded about the club with her Marilyn Monroe voice and mannerisms. I, on the other hand, wore mascara only on my most high-maintenance days, and never even bothered to blow-dry my dishwater-blonde hair. Still, each night, we tallied our table-dance numbers, trying to keep up with one another.

'Well, if he liked me so much, why didn't he get a table dance from me? I went over to him after my set and he barely even looked at me,' she said, stuffing a handful of Doritos in her mouth.

'Don't take it so personal, Grace. Maybe he would rather just sit at the stage than get dances.'

Grace was not fond of rejection. Normally, she could convince even the most reluctant customer to follow her to the table-dance booths. When whispering in their ear and doting on them didn't work, she was not ashamed to pull them playfully by the arms and practically drag them back there. And no man could stay for just one dance with Grace. Even as customers reached for their wallets, determined to cash out, she took them by the face and whispered in their ears. Inevitably, the men would sit back down for another song, and Grace would talk to them – yes, *talk* to them – until the song ended.

'What on earth do you say to them, to get them to stay?' I asked her one night.

'I say, "If you stay, I'll tell you a story."' And that is precisely what she did. I can only imagine what kind of stories she was telling, to get a man to pay $14 just to hear her talk for three minutes.

I dumped the cash on the dressing room floor and began counting it. I couldn't get back to work until I had cashed in all the $1s for $100s.

'I'll help you count,' Grace said, as she grabbed a wad of money from the pile. Together we sat and tallied it all. When we reached the $400 mark, Grace's shoulders began to slump just a little.

'Jeez. He only gave me like $300. What did I do wrong?' she whined.

'Grace, you didn't do anything wrong. You never know... maybe he just liked the fact that I sort of ignored him during my set.'

In the end, we counted over $800. I was thankful to have made more than her, because if the tables had been turned, I would have been asking myself the same question. I tried to comfort her, knowing how she felt. We all tried to wear tough skin and not let it get to us. There were times when we would offer 15 guys in a row a table dance, before one finally said 'Yes'. The girls that made money were the ones who kept asking: the ones who kept risking rejection in hopes that somebody in the club would see something valuable enough in them to spend some money on. Girls like Grace and me heard 'No' a lot. That's how we got 'Yes'. The ones who didn't make money were the ones who let the third and fourth 'No' hurt their feelings.

But even those of us with the toughest skin had nights like Grace was having. No matter how hard I tried to tell myself that none of it was personal, sometimes it still hurt. No matter how much effort I put into convincing myself that just because men seeing me half-naked, with every inch of my body on display, decided that I was not good enough for them to pull $20 out of their pockets didn't reflect on who I was as a woman, sometimes it didn't work.

I tried to look down on the men. I tried to remind myself that outside of the club, most of these guys wouldn't get even a second glance from me, if they tried to talk to me on the street. But sometimes that made it feel even worse. If I let my sense of self get in the way of it all, I was bound to have a crappy night. I would inevitably end up like Grace, pouting in the dressing room and gorging on junk food.

Really, there were two choices: let the rejection reflect on who I was as a woman, or wear a mask. The mask allowed me to pretend that I was someone else; that someone else was getting rejected. Each night, I died, just a little bit, to who I really was. It was just a little bit safer to be someone else.

The night I met Charles, I was prowling the club like a cheetah, hunting for dances. He was sitting in the corner of the club, wearing a blue plaid button-down shirt and khakis. His wrinkled hands were folded and resting on the table near his cola. His thin white hair was trim and neatly combed. I walked by and offered him a table dance. He politely declined.

'No, thank you, honey.' Normally I would have turned up my nose at being called a pet-name like 'honey', but Charles was old, his voice kind and charming.

It was a weeknight, so I picked the songs for my stage performance accordingly. Billie Holiday seemed to be a fitting selection for the lonely businessmen lingering around their airport hotels, looking for something to pass the time. When I stepped onto the stage in my long, sheer black gown, I noticed the white-haired man watching me as he sipped his soda from a straw. In all the years I knew him, Charles never sat at the front of the stage with the other men trying to get a better view of my body. That's not what he was looking for. When my set was over, Charles was waiting near the dressing room door.

'Pardon me. May I please have a dance?' he asked, with a dignified nod of his head.

There was a properness in his voice, as if he were politely asking a classy young woman for a go round on the dance floor at an upscale nightclub.

'Sure. Follow me.' I mirrored his debonair air.

I led Charles up the steps to the well-lit, center booth. By this point in my career as a stripper, I had traded hiding my nakedness in the dark little booths for the brightly lit booths where the other customers could see me, each dance I did serving as an advertisement to potential clients.

'So, what's your name?' I asked, smiling sheepishly and waiting for the song to begin.

'Charles. And you must be Monique…'

'That's me.' I never told them my real name.

'I have a friend named Monique. She used to dance here a long, long time ago. She works in the movies now. I haven't been here since she quit.'

'Oh, really…' I said, pretending to be interested, not knowing that it was a story I would hear again and again for the next couple of years.

During the table dance, Charles smiled nervously; his eyes

dashed about to avoid looking at my body. Charles favored companionship over an erotic show. So I gave him the listening ear and conversation he was looking for, and stuck to harmless and un-telling topics.

'Are you an aspiring actress too?' he asked.

'No. I'm actually a full-time student. I'm getting my degree in psychology.'

'What school do you attend?'

'USC,' I lied. I never gave out information that could be used to track me down outside of the club.

'Ahhh. A Trojan.'

'What about you? What do you do?' I continued the banter.

'Well, honey, I've been retired for quite some time now. I used to work for Boeing.'

'Oh, I see.' I had no idea what Boeing was.

'I started coming here a few years ago, when my wife died.'

'Oh, my gosh, I am so sorry to hear about your wife...'

'She was very sick. Alzheimer's. We were married for 49 years. She died before we made it to our 50-year anniversary.'

He looked off into the distance, and I could see the longing in his eyes. I imagined the anniversary celebration they might have been planning. Adoring friends and family would speak fondly of them, over champagne toasts.

'How sad. I bet you really miss her.'

'Yes, honey, I do. I do a lot of crossword puzzles nowadays... to pass the time. Ever since the other Monique left, there wasn't really a reason for me to come any more.'

The song was over before we knew it. He stayed for a few more dances, and told me he would be back again. And he was. He quickly became a 'regular'. More than a regular, he became a constant. Every Wednesday at 7.30 pm, I could count on seeing Charles sitting in the same third-row chair, sipping on a cola, with at least $300 in his pocket.

He was always respectful of my time. He never expected me to sit around and talk to him outside of the table-dance booth as some of the other girls did with their customers. He paid for my time and asked for nothing more.

'You are one tenacious young lady,' he would often say, in reference to my work ethic. Knowing I was at the club to make money, he was content to pay me $20 every three and a half minutes, just to talk. Sometimes I would run out of things to say, or feel guilty that he was paying so much just for my company, so I would dance for him. But I could see by his averting eyes that he wasn't comfortable. When I was leaning across the table, listening to him repeat stories about his wife or his days working at Boeing, he could pretend that I was a normal friend. Still, I often felt I owed him more than just my presence and words. It was hard to believe that my mere company was enough.

One night, he showed me a picture of himself from when he was 19 years old and had enlisted in the Marines. It was an aged, sepia photo of him in uniform, with his head turned slightly to the side, accentuating a strong jawline. His eyes were sparkling with youth and possibility, and for the first time I realized that he wasn't just an old man; he was a man. A man who had once been handsome; striking, actually. A man who had walked into a room while gasping girls clutched the arms of their friends to steady themselves as they took in the sight of him. Captivated by the picture, and my new perspective of him, I stared at it while we talked for almost an entire song. And from time to time, he would bring the picture to the club again, forgetting I had seen it. Each time, I was as enthralled as the first.

I sprained my ankle while jumping off a small cliff in a paint-balling expedition one weekend, and ended up on crutches for two months. I call it a 'sprain', but it would be more accurate to say that I ripped every tendon and muscle in the bottom half of my leg, leaving it black and blue and brilliant shades of purple from my foot to my knee.

So much for stripping. Instead, I lay on the couch all day and night, watching the entire series of *The Godfather* movies, along with other mafia favorites. I remember feeling sick to my stomach after watching *Casino*. The female lead, played by Sharon Stone, is a classy and beautiful woman with all the luxuries of the world laid at her feet. Still, she finds herself catering to her leeching, no-good, high-school sweetheart.

It made no sense to me that a woman that beautiful would pine after such a scumbag, when he obviously did nothing but hold her back in life. Feelings of nausea and depression lingered during the closing credits. I couldn't understand my reaction to the movie; nor could I shake it. I finally resolved that I must be feeling that way because Sharon Stone's character reminded me of my mother, who once ran the streets of Vegas and found herself trying to squeeze the potential out of more than one man in her lifetime. It took me several years before I finally realized that *I* was the one whom Sharon Stone reminded me of. *I* was the one who was letting my 'leeching, no-good, high-school sweetheart' suck the potential right out of my life.

True to form, Derrick was nowhere to be found in my time of need. It hurt too much to stand long enough to cook anything, so I kept a bag of sourdough bread rolls next to the couch. Derrick seemed to relish my condition, because he was free to gallivant around town with the other women in his life.

Despite all the money I was making, I still had not managed to save any of it. I had long since cleaned out the money in my safety deposit box, after Derrick told me he was in some sort of life-threatening emergency and needed money fast. Whether it was true or not, I handed him the $10,000 I had saved.

When it came time to pay rent, I found myself desperate for money. That's when I decided to call Charles, and drop some not so subtle hints about my situation. He kindly offered to help pay my bills until I could get back to work. Only problem: how would he get the money to me? I had heard enough stories about girls getting stalked by psycho customers that I wouldn't dare give out my address. So, despite my policy not to see customers outside of work, we decided to meet at a neutral location: The Cheesecake Factory in Marina Del Rey. Ever cautious, I brought CoCo, a friend from the club, along the first time. She was a buxom brunette I had rescued from her steroid-charged, abusive boyfriend. On the night I helped her collect her belongings from their luxury apartment, her enraged boyfriend looked me directly in the eye and offered me his venomous wishes.

'I hope you die of AIDs!'

I stood facing him, stunned to silence. An icy chill coursed through my veins.

'Come on, CoCo. Let's get out of here,' I said, trying to appear unaffected by his words. Under the strict rule of her boyfriend, CoCo was used to having the very air she breathed given out in rations. Unacquainted with setting out to live her own life, she was happy to shadow mine. She gladly accompanied me to meet Charles. I didn't think that a kind-hearted, 80-something-year-old man would have much luck doing anything harmful in broad daylight in a public restaurant, but I brought her, just in case.

CoCo and I ordered salads. Charles ordered pork chops, or as he called them, 'poke chops'. I wondered what people were thinking of the two of us sitting with this old man. Did they think we were call girls? I scanned the room for stares and sneers, but there weren't any. Everyone must have thought I was his granddaughter or something. I could have been. And to be honest, sometimes I wished I were. During the hours we spent in the table-dancing booth, I imagined all sorts of scenarios. I wondered what our relationship could have been if we had met somewhere benign, like a park bench or a café. Maybe I would be able to introduce him to my widowed grandmother. They were both so sad and lonely after losing their spouses. Perhaps they could find company and joy in each other. Perhaps they would show the world that it's never too late to fall in love.

But that would never happen. Because no matter how much I dreamed, and how normal our relationship looked at The Cheesecake Factory, I would always be a stripper, and he my customer.

The next time I bent my rules and met a customer outside of the club, I was a little more brazen. He was an educated, middle-aged man with a high-paying job and a fiancée back east. He frequented the club during business trips to Los Angeles. I entertained him with a sassy attitude and philosophical debates. *Is truth universal? And what of the death penalty, euthanasia? What is morality? Who determines it?*

Promised $500 for nothing more than my company at a movie near his hotel room in Marina Del Rey, I showed up in a short, black dress and strappy, black, designer shoes. I was a hired woman, and played the part, throwing my head back in well-timed fits of laughter, and linking my arm in his as we sauntered down the theater's hall.

During the previews to a movie I still can't remember, sitting with my long, freshly shaved legs crossed seductively, I looked around the dimly lit theater. There were couples on dates; a pack of teens out for the night; a family. A family with children. As a child, I had been to this very theater with my grandmother and father, to watch *ET*. It was the first time I remember going to the movies, and I found myself entranced by the adorable alien. Believing he was as real as the hair on my head, I left a small dish of Reece's Pieces on my front porch each night, hoping he would visit me one day. The innocence of this memory overwhelmed me.

I turned to my 'date': 'I need to use the restroom. I'll be right back.'

Still playing my part in spite of myself, I walked to the restroom, switching my hips, taking long smooth strides all the way. How else would I walk in those heels? The bathroom was stark white and empty, and it smelled of stale urine and floral air freshener. Prepared to pretend I was washing my hands should someone walk in, I studied my image in the mirror, and confronted the woman before me with a question. It was the same one I posed the night I auditioned to work at the club.

'Who are you?'

I had no answer. I was more than one person. I was Monique. I was Harmony. I was some combination of the two, and I wasn't quite sure who *either* of them was.

I thought back to an afternoon when I was about ten years old. I was with my mother, driving down Lincoln Boulevard in Venice, when we stopped for a stringy-headed blonde woman in a saggy tank top and micro miniskirt. Holding out her thumb, she appeared to be hitch-hiking.

'Get in,' my mother offered kindly. There was a smile on her face and a knowing look in her eyes that told me she was up to something. I climbed to the back of our red van to make room for our new passenger. I couldn't make out the look that crossed her face as she took in the sight of me. Was it confusion? Fear?

Nevertheless, she slid into the car timidly, and focused intently on some nothing outside it.

'Where ya headed?' my mother asked, still smiling with her eyes.

'Uh… Um… You can just drop me off down the way.' She wrung her wiry hands together in her lap, and it occurred to me that she didn't have a destination at all. My mother had picked up a prostitute.

There was a thick silence, and in it an exchange between my mother and this woman. My mother seemed to know her: not personally, by name, but intimately by circumstance. I sat watching them in their quiet stand-off, waiting for something to happen.

'You can just let me out here,' the woman said, when we reached Venice Boulevard.

And just like that, she was gone. I moved back to the front seat, taking the place where the woman had been sitting, and fixed my gaze on the passing sidewalk.

'Mom, why did you pick her up?' I finally asked.

'Do you know what she was doing?' my mother said, in her wise, lesson-giving voice.

'She was a prostitute, right?'

'That's right. The oldest profession in the book.'

The oldest profession in the book. That is what my mother always said when she talked about prostitutes; only I never knew what book she was referring to. Her tone told me that this book and its mention of prostitution as the first profession made it viable and therefore above criticism.

'Yeah, but why did you pick her up?' I asked again.

My mother quietly stared out of the front windshield. She seemed to be seeing the same nothing that the prostitute had. She never answered my question. Looking at myself in that movie-theater bathroom, just blocks from where my mother and I had dropped the woman off years ago, I wondered what separated me from her. How was I different? Was I different because at the end of the night I would turn down this man's request to accompany him to his hotel room? Was I different because, when customers offered me thousands of dollars to give them a piece of myself, I threw my nose in the air and proudly declared that I was not a prostitute? If I was so different, so much better, then why did I feel the same?

Three
STRIPPED

JUST WHEN THE CATERPILLAR THOUGHT THE WORLD WAS OVER,
IT BECAME A BUTTERFLY.

Anonymous

'Mowwwwwnick…' Jade said, as she shoved her locker closed and spun towards me.

'Jaaaaaade…' I bantered.

'Have you seen Jasmine's implants?' Jade's eyebrows, which were permanently tattooed into perfect black arches, were raised mischievously as she initiated the gossip. Anyone who wasn't in the locker room was fair game for being talked about.

'Umm… yeah. How could I miss them, Jade?' I replied, as I sprayed myself with vanilla body spray from the neck down.

'They look crazy! They're completely lopsided!' Summer chimed in, while scrunching her long brown locks in the mirror. 'Do you think she realizes how bad they look?'

'How could she not?' Jade giggled.

'She says she makes more money now, though. The customers are apparently too dumb to notice. And Lucy is making more money now, too, since she got hers,' I offered.

'Yeah, but Lucy always made good money, Mownick.'

'If I were Jasmine, I'd take those things back! I'd get myself a refund on them things!' Summer said, slapping her muscly little thighs and wiggling her tiny hips. We all exploded into laughter.

'That's why I'm getting mine done by Dr Preston. I've heard

he's the best, and every girl he's done has looked really good.'

'What! Monique? You're not getting implants, are you?' Grace had been quiet up to this point, sitting primly on the carpet with her legs neatly placed to one side. A buffet of snacks was laid out before her.

'Why wouldn't I? I have an appointment next week. I'm ready to up my game and make some more money around here,' I noted, ignoring evidence to the contrary. Grace and I were two of the top earners at the club and two of the few girls who didn't have implants. But each time I had a hard night and faced the rejection of tight-pocketed clients, I heard the voices we all did. *It's your outfit... your hair. If your breasts were bigger, your waist smaller, your body more tanned, teeth whiter, heels higher... maybe then they would like you.*

'Oh, Monique, please don't. You're beautiful just the way you are,' Grace said as she brushed a few strands of her platinum hair away from her fire-engine-colored, glossy lips, leaving faint red streaks across her porcelain cheeks.

'Don't worry, Grace. I'm not getting them huge. Just a full C. Very natural.' 'Natural' was the word of choice when girls described the kind of implants they were going to get; yet I had seldom seen an implant that looked very natural at all.

'Monique, I want to tell you a story,' Grace said in her sweet, Marilyn Monroe voice. It was the same voice and line she used to lure her clients into staying for another dance.

'OK. But I only have a couple minutes, 'cuz I have to get back to work.'

Jade stood behind Grace and rolled her eyes, as if to say, 'Here we go again,' before walking out of the locker room.

Grace cleared a place on the carpet next to her and handed me a bag of gummy bears. She proceeded to tell me about a time when she went under the knife and walked away with a new set of 'reasonably sized' Ds. She felt great about the thousands of dollars spent, until the first day she went back to the Saturday morning ballet class she took to stay graceful and fit.

'I looked at myself in the mirror, with all of the other dancers – so long and sleek – and I immediately regretted my decision. I missed my delicate little B-sized chest,' she said, as she stretched her neck and torso. 'So I went back and had them removed.' Grace lifted her bikini to reveal the tender pink scars she bore from repeated surgery.

The next week, on the day of my appointment, I remembered Grace's scars. I stood in front of the mirror and examined my décolletage without regard for the opinions of men or the desire for money. I readjusted my posture, held my head up high and did an arabesque. I supposed implants would look pretty silly in ballet class. So I skipped my appointment with Dr Preston and signed up for a ballet class.

I stood at the ballet bar with my pale pink tights and black leotard, tucking my pelvis in tightly and elongating my spine as I assumed first position. It felt good to be in a dance class again. To wear ballet clothes, as I had when I was a little girl at the Westside Academy of Dance, where a stuffy woman in a knee-length skirt played the piano for us to dance to. My ballet teacher vied for my attention as I twirled around the room, but I continued to dance with little regard for choreography or instruction.

'Harmony, the rest of the class is doing jetés,' she would call out to me.

Plié–leap–spin–bounce–hop–hop–twirl. I was lost in a world where I was princess over all the land and an adoring audience looked on, while I danced in the fluffiest tutu the world had ever seen. Little girls don't wake up one day and dream of being a stripper. They don't close their eyes and wish to find a man who will call them names and sleep with other women. I had hopes of living in a castle landscaped with white lilies and yellow daffodils. My prince would brush the hair from the nape of my neck and kiss me gently.

I glanced at my grown-up reflection in the mirror at the front of the class and wondered who I could have been if I had stayed in ballet class for all those years. Would my life be different if I had stuck with it, instead of dropping out after an older boy in the class molested me at his birthday slumber party? I told my mom I didn't want to dance any more, and held my ground even when she bribed me with mint chocolate-chip ice cream.

'Tondue,' the teacher called out to the class, and I slid my pink ballet shoe out in front of me at her instruction. The grown-up Harmony followed her direction.

'Front–side–back–side,' the instructor repeated rhythmically. I engaged every muscle in my leg in the movement, from my hip flexors to the tip of my big toe.

The girl in front of me was long and lean, with a waist as delicate as a teacup. Her thick black hair was as shiny as Wonder Woman's. She was as graceful as the little ballerinas my mother used to decorate my birthday cake with, when I was a child.

'Other side,' the teacher said, still in time with the music. The entire class pivoted on relevé and faced the other direction.

'Nice arch,' a kind voice commented from behind. I glanced over my shoulder at the cake-top-ballerina girl to make sure she was talking to me. She was.

'Thanks. Great turn out,' I noted. Her feet were beautifully positioned at 180 degrees.

'Thanks.' She smiled vibrantly, revealing bright white teeth between perfect plum lips.

As the class continued, my arms ached from holding them in various ballet positions for so long. 'Oh my gosh, my arms are about to fall off,' I grunted under my breath, and the girl burst into giggles. When the teacher looked to see what the commotion was about, we both straightened up and made serious faces. This of course made us want to giggle again. Holding it in only made us laugh even harder. I knew instantly I was dealing with a fellow class clown. This should be fun, I thought.

'Hi, I'm Tanya,' she said when class was over. Her eyes were gleaming.

'Harmony. Nice to meet you.' I had to think twice before I introduced myself. I had become more and more accustomed to calling myself Monique, and I didn't want to use the wrong name by accident.

From that point on, we stood next to each other at the ballet bar and continued our antics, much to the teacher's chagrin. I found myself showing up to class a few minutes early, hoping to chat with her. There was something about Tanya. All it took was one glance, and we both wanted to start laughing. She made me feel young again.

One day after class, Tanya asked me the question I dreaded the most.

'So, what do you do?'

'You mean for work?' I stammered.

'Yeah… for work.' Her eyes were so warm and kind, I didn't want to lie to her.

'Um… I'm a dancerhowaboutyou?' I quickly evaded further discussion, failing to mention what sort of dance I did.

On the way home, I re-played the conversation in my head. I wondered if I should have told her the entire truth? I told myself it wasn't really her business what I did for a living; still, I didn't want to begin our friendship on a lie. In the end, I decided that I needed to tell her the truth. Since I had been dancing, she was the first person I felt like being completely honest with. Maybe it was because she had mentioned something about going to church. I think I felt guilty about lying to a churchgoer. Maybe

I thought that if she had an 'in' with God, she would find out about it anyway.

I was nervous about telling her, because I thought coming clean might mean that she wouldn't want to talk to me any more – after all, she was a Christian. I didn't know much about Christians, but I was pretty sure they didn't like strippers.

Either I was wrong, or Tanya was not like other Christians. She loved me anyway. What's more, she seemed to actually *like* me. All of those years I had spent hearing Derrick's voice pointing out my every flaw, telling me that I was stupid and annoying and that nobody else would ever want to be with me, had made me forget that there was anything about me *worth* liking. The fact that someone as beautiful and kind as Tanya laughed at my jokes and wanted to spend time with me made me feel special. Through her eyes, I started to see myself differently.

The lights went out in the table-dance booth and I stood up to drop another token in the token machine. Once again, warm red light illuminated the booth. I resumed my position, sitting on a beach towel I had spread out on the floor, at eye level with Charles.

'Forty-nine years we were married. Almost made it to our golden anniversary,' Charles said, as if for the first time, looking longingly into his glass of cola. I had heard it before, but he needed to say it again. His short-term memory continued to decline, and he needed to keep the memory of her fresh. I gently pulled the cloudy spectacles from his face and cleaned them with the hem of my skirt.

'She used to play the piano…'

'What did she play?' I asked, replacing his glasses and resting my chin on top of clasped hands.

He sat back in his seat and frowned as he tried to remember.

'Well, honey, I can't think of it right now, but when she was alive, our entire home was filled with beautiful music.'

Her absence was an ever-present force in his life. He clung to the memory of her. He clung to anything that felt familiar. That is why he chose me in the first place; I shared the stage name of the first dancer he ever visited after his wife died. Monique. It was familiar. He could remember that.

Charles had a hole. It was the space that the love of his life once occupied. Try as he might, he couldn't fill it. Sure, he enjoyed my company; but most of all, I believe he enjoyed reliving the memory of his wife: reliving what it felt like to have the company of a woman.

It seemed that the men at the club all had holes. They were searching to fulfill legitimate needs. The overworked businessman with no time for a personal life; the socially awkward nerd who never felt comfortable with women; the flashy type, flaunting cash to feel powerful; the guy-next-door, an average, slightly dissatisfied man looking for something to fill time and space. They all had holes. Charles's hole was endearing to me.

I had a hole, too, and an insatiable thirst to have it filled. I longed for someone to see past the scars and stilettos; beyond the façade of glamour; to find the woman locked deep inside me. I sensed her presence when I sat at the foot of the ocean and fathomed its vastness; when I peeked inside the windows of quaint houses filled with happy families and dreamed I belonged in one of them. I could feel her inside me, willing me to survive long enough to find a force powerful enough to unleash her, to set her free.

Twenty-One

My grandmother and I were walking out the door of my West Los Angeles apartment when the phone rang. I knew I had to answer it. If it was Derrick calling, he would blow a gasket if I didn't. After he had finished interrogating me about my whereabouts, he would punish me with the silent treatment and not answer my calls for days.

'I have to get that,' I said, as I ran back in the house to grab the phone.

'Hello?' I said hurriedly.

'Hey, Harmony!' It was Tanya. The muscles in my shoulders relaxed.

'I know this is last-minute, but we are having a special at church tonight, with singers and comedians, and I was wondering if you wanted to come,' she offered.

Tanya had been inviting me to visit her church for the past few months, but waking up early on a Sunday morning after working as late as 4.00 am was never on my agenda. Besides, I wasn't too sure I liked the idea of going to church.

When I didn't take her up on her offer to go to church, she invited me to coffee or frozen yogurt instead. I didn't feel as if I was some sort of goody-two-shoes project she was working on: trying to get brownie points with God for getting a girl like me to show up on a Sunday. She showed interest in getting to know me, whether I went to church with her or not. I looked across the room at my grandmother, standing regally in her pale lavender slacks and matching shirt adorned with a hand-painted zebra.

'Now, Harmony, isn't this just darling!' she had said as she pulled the ensemble out of her suitcase earlier that day.

Ever since she came to town to visit me, I had been searching for ways to entertain her. Her favorite things to do were to eat, shop, and walk. So far, we had been doing plenty of all three. In true Grandma Mary form, at breakfast we would talk about what we were going to have for lunch. This always included 'freshhhh vegetables', which she said emphasizing their freshness, even if they were canned. At lunch we would discuss dinner, and perhaps breakfast for the next day, and of course where we could find some cute places to shop. This was all interspersed with long walks throughout the neighborhood, to burn off all the calories we had consumed. During the walks, my grandmother took the opportunity to reinforce the goodness of exercise. She also stopped to appreciate the various flowers, trees and shrubbery. I had walked through my neighborhood on countless occasions, but somehow I had neglected to notice the tree with gorgeous white trumpet-shaped flowers, or the wonderful lemon smell of lilac-colored roses. My grandmother saw it all, and she helped me see it too.

And although we were still full from lunch, we were on our way out to have dinner at a promising-looking café we had spotted earlier in the week. I figured dinner could wait. A church event was just the sort of thing that would entertain my Grandma.

'Grandma, it's Tanya, and she is inviting us to a special thing at her church tonight. Do you want to go?' I asked.

'Well, why not?' she said, with an exuberant smile, hardly disguising excitement that her grandbaby was finally going to set foot in a church.

We hopped into my green Honda Civic and drove down Robertson Boulevard at dashing speeds. My grandmother was not one to arrive fashionably late to anything, particularly not a church event, so on this one occasion she did her best not to make grunting noises and squeeze her eyes shut every time I tapped the brake, fearing I would get us into a fatal crash. She sucked up the fear that comes with seeing a person whose diapers you have changed sit behind the wheel of an engine-powered, thousand-pound hunk of metal, and let me run the yellow lights.

'Now, Harmony, what time are we supposed to be there?' she urged in her East Texas accent, willing me to drive faster.

We were in such a rush to get there that I almost forgot to be nervous. Suddenly, I remembered my experience at a church service two years before, during a family reunion. Naturally, that Sunday, the entire town of Winnsboro, Texas, went to church. It also happened to be Father's Day. And as fate would have it, my father and I were both at the reunion that year. It was the only time I can remember being in the same state with him on Father's Day. While the rest of the world celebrated fatherhood with silly, sentimental Hallmark cards addressed to the Number 1 Greatest Dad, who, with patience and consistency, taught his children everything he knew about life and the world at large, I walked up and down the aisles of card shops for what felt like hours, searching for something that would capture the sentiments I held toward my father with a remote sense of honesty. Greeting card companies have yet to make a card that says, 'It was good to see you the other year; hope you will call for Christmas again. Enjoy Father's Day.'

Over the years, I had discovered that my safest bet was one of those cards that had humorous clippings from *The Far Side* comics on the front and a very simple message on the inside: 'Happy Father's Day.'

Normally, at the family reunions, much to my grandmother's chagrin, I would stay behind while the rest of the family went to the little white church house for their Sunday fix. 'What am I supposed to do when everyone goes to church?' I asked my mother when I was a kid. 'You don't have to go to church if you don't want to. And you can just tell them that I said so.' So that's what I normally did.

But that time, with it being Father's Day and all, I wanted to go, just to see what it would be like to have a dad around. My dad and I sat next to each other in the service and listened to the preacher man talk about, of all things, *fatherhood*! He spoke directly to all of the fathers in the room about what it means to be a father, noting how significant fathers are in the life of a child.

I don't think I could imagine anything more embarrassing than sitting next to my father for something like that. My grandmother kept glancing over at my father, hoping he was listening. And I was certain that everyone in the room was looking too, knowing that we hadn't seen each other in years and that we had totally screwed up the whole father–daughter thing. The more the preacher talked about what a family was supposed to look like, the more convinced I became that I had no place in church.

Fifteen minutes later, we were driving slowly along Wilshire Boulevard, scanning the building numbers for the address Tanya had given me. I finally found it, but the church looked nothing like the quaint little chapel in Winnsboro. It was a converted movie house, with 1920s architecture, and the word 'Oasis' written across the top in bold, modern lettering. We pulled into the parking lot across the street, and I sat looking at the church in my rear-view mirror.

'OK, Harmony, let's go…' My grandmother was already out of the car, with her purse hanging on her shoulder.

I got out of the car and tugged at the bottom of my fitted slate-grey skirt. I realized I should have changed before we left the house. I could have come up with something churchier to wear than this, like my ankle-length floral dresses. I wondered whether people in church even showed their knees. I remembered my mom telling me something about people being hit with rulers by nuns for showing their kneecaps.

My grandmother, who wasn't one for moseying, bounded towards the church. 'Don't tell me you can't keep up with an ol' woman!' she said, challenging me. I fell for it every time. Quickening my pace, a speedwalking race ensued as we rushed to the church doors. We arrived to find a large auditorium filled with turquoise, movie-theater-style seats, where an usher wearing a tan suit seated us.

The church was nothing like what I expected. From what I knew, there were white churches and black churches, and nothing in between. The white churches I saw on television had their monotone hymnals, lacy doilies, and self-contained preachers. The black churches had their hat-wearing, fan-waving, aisle-dancing passionate outbursts. Their preachers growled requests for Amens and Hallelujahs. Their sermons were almost musical, each point emphasized by outbursts from the choir or a chord played by the organist.

And, of course, the black churches had gospel. If there was one thing that made me want to believe in God, it was gospel music. Just to get a taste of it, I would watch my favorite scene in *The Color Purple* over and over again. It was the scene where Shug Avery, a sultry blues singer, walks up a dirt trail and wails, 'I couldn't sleep at all last night… And I was wondering why…' Then she bursts into the doors of a church where her father is preaching, lamenting that *maybe God is trying to tell them something*. The preacher had given up on his wayward daughter, but she came to tell him that God loves sinners – even blues singers. I loved her, too.

The gems of my music collection were old, unmarked tapes containing music from various massed choirs. When I was all alone, I would pull the blinds closed in my dreary little living room, and to these voices I performed the most graceful lyrical dances that I possibly could. When no one else could see, I made a connection with generations of singers who all shared one thing in common: they loved a man named Jesus. And though I didn't share their love for Him, I loved the way *they* loved Him. On some days, just that was enough for me to get by.

Sometimes I thought about going to church, but I was faced with a dilemma. I am white.

My mother would beg to differ. A follower of the Red Path, she clings to the traces of Native American blood coursing through our veins. But to all intents and purposes, I am white. And I don't like doilies and quiet hymnals, like they had in the white churches on TV.

At Tanya's church the whole idea of a 'white' or 'black' church faded. It was simply a room full of people who felt like family. Effortless. I imagined that if there was such a place as heaven, it was liable to look a lot closer to this than the homogeneous church I was familiar with.

A woman stepped onto the platform. 'Let's worship together,' she said exuberantly, in a voice that was not quite a shout. Conversations trailed, and the people in the room rose and began clapping. I followed the woman's cue and fell in love at first note. Her vibrato-inflected voice was rich and belting.

'Now this is what I call a tushie-waggin' church,' my grandmother leaned over and said in her usual, way-too-loud whisper. She was referring to the beat-keeping, side-stepping congregation. Being Southern Baptist, she wasn't allowed to wag her tushie, or any other body part for that matter.

Even though my grandmother was just about as rebellious as they come, according to the standards of people born in the Deep South in 1918, we were a little out of her element. She was the first in her family to leave Winnsboro behind for the big city, where she got a job as a mail carrier for the US Postal Service in Dallas. She was featured in the papers as being the first ever female government employee. Besides being dangerously independent, she did all sorts of frowned-upon things such as card playing and cocktail sipping. Still, the fact that this church was not as much to my grandmother's liking as I had hoped made me like it even more.

During the next song, a ballad of sorts, the people weren't singing *about* Jesus; they seemed to be singing *to* Him. Their eyes were closed, and many sang with reaching, hoping hands, raised as if there was something to be grasped right there on the ceiling of the room. Others had their palms outstretched, as if they were waiting to receive some intangible thing.

I clasped my hands in front of my heart and swayed to the music. Then I noticed an attractive woman with tumbling tresses of red hair a row ahead. She wore a sensible, beige two-piece suit, and looked like the kind of woman who had a steady boyfriend and held down a good job. Her hands were drawn to her chin, which rested gently on them. She didn't look sad, but she was crying, as if she had been captivated by something wonderful. Longing to go to that place, I closed my eyes just to see if it was possible. In that room, as I allowed myself to experience this thing called worship, somehow I understood I had finally come home.

I looked at the clock behind the bar: 10.00 pm. It was a late start, leaving me with some catching up to do. My life was so busy it seemed as if I was always running behind. Every day I went to school, persevering with my determined efforts to take all the classes I needed to transfer to University of California at Los Angeles and finish my Bachelor's degree in psychology. I spent my nights off studying. Then, every Wednesday, I went to the seven o'clock service at Oasis, going in later to work at the club. Management had been letting it slide.

I had grown to love church. Each time I went, it felt like the pastor was speaking directly to me. As if we were the only two people in the room, and he knew everything I had been going through and exactly what I needed to hear.

I wanted to be at church every time the doors were opened, but it was starting to feel weird going to church and coming to my shift at the strip club afterwards. After hearing this uplifting message, hugging all of these nice people who asked me about my day and how school was going, I would show up to work at the club. They were such different worlds, and I was having a hard time figuring out how to live in both of them. A couple of times after church, I started driving towards the club and turned my car around. I just couldn't bring myself to go there. It was getting harder and harder to show up. I decided I needed to get my schedule changed.

Standing at the bar, I scanned the room to see a small-framed Middle Eastern man wearing heavy gold jewelry walk in. He was escorted by what appeared to be a bodyguard, a large man in a black suit wearing a stoic expression as he clutched a black leather briefcase in his hands. They were heading towards the bar, so I stayed put, hoping to score some table dances. Before I even had a chance to approach them, the bodyguard walked directly to me and asked me to dance for the man he was protecting. That was easy, I thought to myself.

'Hi there. My name is Monique. What's yours?' I said, wearing a sugary smile as we walked over to the booths. He gave me his name, but I didn't listen.

I thought about playing my 'accent joke' on him. The one where, wearing the most dingbat expression I could muster, I would ask a guy with an obviously British accent, 'Are you from

Texas?' After I asked the question I would stare blankly, ever amused by their reaction.

Some men didn't seem surprised; as if I was simply reinforcing their stereotype of me. Most would chuckle to themselves and politely tell me where they were from, and of course it was never Texas. I didn't let them in on my private joke; I enjoyed letting them think I was a dumb blonde. I decided not to play the accent joke on the Middle Eastern man and simply moved on to my next line of small talk.

'So, where are you from?'

He told me where he was from. I didn't listen.

'Oh really,' I said, feigning interest.

'Take a seat.' His bodyguard stood several feet away from us. Just far enough to give us privacy, but still close enough to do his job. As I dropped a token into the coin machine to illuminate the booth, I felt the red lights wash over me. I swayed around in front of him and slowly peeled off my dress, and I noticed that he was focusing on my face. I made a seductive half-turn so that I could keep my back to him for a moment, to break his gaze. Please stop looking at my face, I begged silently. And at that moment I felt something in me break ever so slightly, and I wanted to cry.

I was so tired of being looked at. I was tired of coming to this club and dealing with all these men. I began to ponder the concept of purpose my pastor had been talking about. This can't be God's plan for me, I thought. I wanted to break down, and I could taste the salty onset of a big cry rising in the back of my throat. OK, Harmony, you have to hold it together, I told myself. I couldn't let myself fall apart right there in the table-dance booth, so I swallowed hard and lifted my head to keep the tears from falling.

The DJ faded out the Celine Dion song that had been

playing. Before the lights in the booth automatically turned off, I bent down and routinely asked the man if he wanted another dance. Without saying a word, he made a circular motion with his index finger as if he were ordering another round of drinks. Round two. And when the second song was over, he ordered another round. And another, and another.

I had a repertoire of choreography that could get me through about four table dances without repeating any moves. After that, I improvised. After ten songs had passed, he waved his hand, beckoning me to his level.

'Do you like your job?' he asked in his thick accent.

'Yeah; it gets me through school.' I offered my automated response.

'I am paying my way through school' was a standard response from most girls in the club, but I was one of the few who were actually enrolled. Many started out with the intention of finishing, before 'taking a semester off' to save up money. One semester turned to two, and so on. Then came the reasoning, 'Why do I need a degree, when I can make more money than most attorneys working at the club?'

Degrees last, looks don't, was my reasoning. Take Lola. She was beautiful once, and still is if you don't use strip club standards. With thick black hair and olive skin, she was shaped like the Chiquita Banana girl and had the same swagger about her. But Lola was in her fifties and had to wear thigh-high stockings with a garter belt to disguise her varicose veins. She had been at the club since her twenties. I wondered if she had started out like me, thinking she would only do it for a couple of months to pay off some debt or other. Now, literally decades later, in order to compete with the younger girls for the customers' attention, she had to do more, give more, always pushing her boundaries. In the dressing room the other girls called her dirty. 'Did you see what

Lola was doing with that guy? She's nasty!' they gossiped. She had to do something to compete with the 16-year-olds working on fake IDs.

What else could Lola do? No employable skills, no résumé. Stripping was all she knew.

'Yes, you pay for school, but do you like your job?' the client repeated, with his head tilted and eyebrows raised.

Just then, the bodyguard walked over and whispered something in his ear. The customer looked up and waved the bodyguard away. Then he leaned back in his chair and crossed his legs, before addressing me. 'I have a plane to catch. I am returning home. But first I must speak to you. You should come home with me to my country – tonight,' he added.

I had to play my cards right. A quick 'No' would send the man straight to the airport, meaning no more dances; no more money. There was a better way of doing this. My strategy was to make him think I was considering his offer, so he would stick around to convince me to leave with him.

'Be quiet. You don't really want me to fly home with you,' I said sheepishly, as I dropped another token in the coin machine.

'I am serious. You would have a very nice life. You could be my wife,' the man offered.

I would have thought he was kidding, but his hard black eyes told me he was not the kind of man that joked around. I remembered the story my mother had told me, about an Arabian Prince who approached her on the Boardwalk when I was a toddler. He offered to buy me from her – to raise me as his wife! I wondered if this man was raising any wives back home. I decided to shift gears.

'How could I leave tonight? I don't even have my bags packed.' The longer the dialogue continued, the more money I would make.

'I would give you everything you need. You won't need a suitcase,' he countered.

'But what about my education?'

'There will always be school. I am offering you a new life.' He looked me directly in the eye.

'You're serious?' It was more of an observation than a question. This man was offering me a new life. 'Everything you need.' Those were his words. Frankly, I could use a new life. I was quite tired of the one I was living. I wondered what Derrick would think if I suddenly disappeared. How long would it take before he gave up trying to find me? How long would he wait before he found some other woman to meet all his needs?

I was beginning to realize that I really *did* want a new life. But not the one that this man was offering. For the next 10 or 15 songs, I presented him with all the challenges that hopping on a plane and moving to another country might pose. As long as he thought that I was considering his offer carefully, he would stay and buy more table dances.

'I have already missed my first plane. You must decide,' he finally said abruptly. He was getting frustrated.

'I just don't know,' I whined sweetly.

Running out of stall tactics, I began to dance for him again. I had been reasoning with and dancing for him for 42 songs straight, and my feet throbbed in their six-inch stilettos. The bodyguard returned.

'I must go before I miss another plane. I wish you would come with me.' He gave it one last shot.

'I'm sorry; I just can't,' I said, turning his offer down once and for all.

He tossed his hands up in surrender and pushed his chair back.

'How much?' he asked.

'Well, let's see… you have had 55 dances…' I lied, tacking on a few extra. 'That will be \$825… not including tip.'

He motioned for the bodyguard, who placed the briefcase on the table and unlatched it. As it flipped open, I caught a glimpse of stacks and stacks of American money.

The client stood up and began walking away, as the bodyguard handed me a stack of crisp hundred-dollar bills: \$1,200. Watching them walk out, I wondered what my life would be like if I had followed. I could throw on some clothes, grab my purse and start all over in some foreign country, where I was wined and dined like royalty. Or I could end up locked in this man's basement somewhere, held captive as a sex slave. I had heard of that happening: American girls being invited to a foreign country with the promise of good money, only to be held captive and their documents stolen. I would have to find a safer way to start a new life.

You too can make \$4.75 an hour, I thought to myself, as I slipped my time card in the little machine behind the bar.

'What's up, Monique?' Gabe slapped his hand on my shoulder as he turned the corner.

'Minimum wage. I just can't get over the fact that we get paid minimum wage. That just sounds degrading,' I vented.

Gabe rolled his eyes and shook his head. 'Are you kidding me? We're the only strip club I know of that even pays the dancers *any* sort of hourly fee. Think of it as a bonus,' he argued.

Of course, everyone made more than that. Even the girls who sat in the dressing room all night could pull in at least \$40, if they went on stage a couple of times.

'I guess you're right. \$4.75 is still \$4.75 more than I have. Hey, I need to talk to Tony about my schedule.'

'I'll let 'em know,' Gabe replied, as he hurried off to the back office.

As I walked away, I noticed a flier with a picture of a little girl above the time cards. It must have taken a half a can of hairspray to get her bangs that high. They were perched on top of her head like a tidal wave. *Missing. Last seen April 1, 1991.*

At the time the picture was taken, she was ten years old. She would have been at least 16 years old by now. I wondered who would have thought to put this flier up in a strip club. Did they have a reason to think she would be here? *Had she been here, in this club?*

I couldn't stop looking at her, and the way her little arm hung over the side of the black cocker spaniel nestled beneath her. She was caught in a moment, smiling. Not for the camera, but for the person taking the picture. What could she have been running from? Or *to*, for that matter? What kinds of things do ten-year-olds do to survive on their own? It was all too sad to think about.

'Come on, Monique.' Gabe waved me into Tony's office across from the bar.

'Have a seat,' Tony said, pointing to an office chair next to his cluttery desk. His 'office' was an enormous room that used to be a part of the bowling alley before the place became a strip club. It was filled with old bar stools, chairs with rips in the seats, and even a couple of inoperable bowling lanes.

Tony continued ruffling though the papers on his desk as he waited for me to speak. His thick, shiny mane of black hair was smoothed back meticulously. In the years I had worked there, I rarely interacted with Tony, who stayed tucked away behind his desk every night. We girls spoke to him face to face only when we needed time off or schedule changes. The rest of the time, he communicated through floor managers.

'Hi, Tony, how are you?' I began.

'I'm fine, Monique. How are you?' he said, in his faint New

York-Italian accent. He knew I wanted something.

'Well, I wanted to talk to you about my shift. I need to be taken off the schedule on Wednesdays.' I crossed my legs and swished my chair from side to side.

'Nobody wants to work weeknights. Everyone wants to work weekends, but nobody wants to work weeknights,' he complained. His two front teeth protruded slightly, resting gently on his plump bottom lip.

'I'll work Tuesdays. I just need to take Wednesdays off.'

'School?' He tapped a stack of paper against the desk and looked up at me.

'No.' I paused, hoping he wouldn't need any further explanation.

'So what is it, then?' He tilted his head slightly, as if to lend me his ear.

'OK, this might sound crazy…' – I nervously adjusted the strap of my powder-blue minidress – '…but I need to be taken off the schedule so I can go to church.'

Tony let out a chuckle. 'That doesn't sound crazy!'

'It doesn't?' I was relieved.

'No, not at all. I go to church, too. My wife and I attend an evening service on Sundays.'

'Really!?' No wonder Tony wasn't interested in spending time on the floor and flirting with all the girls. He was a church guy!

'Yep, really.' He just sat there for a moment, smiling and nodding, as if he was seeing me for the first time. 'All right, then,' he finally said, as he swiveled his chair and returned to business.

'So, does that mean you're approving my schedule?'

'Yes, I'm approving it.'

The alarm sounded at 9.00 am. My body protested, getting up to turn it off. A pounding hangover headache was my only motivation to stop the beeping. The room smelled like stale alcohol and morning breath. I looked over, to see the guy I met in the VIP room at a Jon B concert the night before passed out with his mouth agape in the bed next to me. He was still wearing his dark blue jeans and grey button-down from the night before. Bringing him all the way back to my apartment had seemed like a good idea when we were making out at the concert. But once we were alone in my bedroom, without the blasting music and Long Island iced teas, I ditched the party-girl persona and re-employed my defenses.

'Here are the ground rules: you can sleep here, but you have to stay on your side of the bed and you better not try to touch me in the middle of the night.' He probably thought I was crazy, leading him on the way I had and then flipping it like that.

My heart plummeted into my large intestine at the mere idea of Derrick finding out. When he had talked me into putting him up in his own apartment, saying he needed the extra space now that he was a father, he had no idea that it would lead to this. Just weeks ago, he had given me this whole speech about how I was disrespecting him simply by hugging the people I met at church.

'That's just how we greet each other,' I reasoned with him. 'It doesn't mean anything. Everyone hugs. It would be weird not to.'

'I don't care what you say. It's disrespectful for you to go around hugging people like that. You need to stop.' His tone was firm.

I wanted to smart-mouth him; it's not like I ever get any hugs from you, I thought. Outside of sex, we almost never had any physical contact. In the time I had known him, Derrick had only hugged me once: warm and brief. I wanted to remember everything about that hug: the way my arms felt around his slender waist; my head resting timidly on his clavicle; holding my breath, hoping if I didn't move it would last longer. In a moment, it was over.

As if his lack of affection wasn't enough, he never fully committed to me. He was always running around with other women. Yet he expected my unrelenting devotion. Still, I knew the rules, and I had never dared to break them before. He shot me a glance and I knew it was time to stop talking. One minute I am trying to decide if I should hug other people; the next, I am lying in bed next to a complete stranger.

'Hey!' I tapped him on the shoulder. 'Hey, you've gotta get up.'

'What time is it?' he asked, without opening his eyes.

'It's 9.00 am.' I could feel vomit rising in my throat. 'I've gotta get out of here. It's time to go.'

I had been planning on going to San Diego with Tanya – to see her friends perform – for weeks. Just the thought of riding in a car for an hour and a half agitated my nausea, but I wanted to keep my word to her. I respected her. She made me want to be a better person; to make better choices. As I lay in bed, I realized that the night before had been a step in the wrong direction. I whispered in my head, 'God, I'm so sorry about last night. Please forgive me, and give me the strength to go to San Diego.'

I met Tanya at her friend's house later that morning. The West Los Angeles air was fresh and crisp. When I got into the back seat of René's blue Nissan Pathfinder, I wondered if they could smell the alcohol escaping from my pores. I hoped that the perfume I used was enough to mask it. On the ride to San Diego, I hid my tired, achy eyes behind sunglasses, hoping Tanya's friends, Jason and René, wouldn't notice how hung over

I was. The California Mountains were dry and looming, needing rain. I fought back nausea with each sway and bump of the car. What would they think of me if I threw up all over myself? Just picturing us pulled over on the side of the road using old towels to wipe up my puke made me feel hot with embarrassment.

René was steady and silent throughout the ride. He seemed like the kind of guy you would appoint as a designated driver on a night out. Level-headed, content to sit back and watch things unfold. Aaliyah's 'Are You That Somebody?' came on the radio, and he turned up the volume.

'This song's the shit!' I called out from the back seat, and quickly slapped my hand over my mouth. I didn't mean to cuss in front of church people. I looked up at Tanya, to see how badly I had offended them. She didn't seem fazed. In fact, I am pretty sure I heard Jason giggle in the front seat. And that put me at ease.

'So, what kind of music do you guys do?' I tried to make small talk.

'Hip-hop,' Jason replied, turning to look at me from the front seat. His hair was combed forward and edged neatly, just like Jon B's. Funny, he actually looks like him, I thought to myself.

'Hip-hop? For real?' Christians rapping. This should be interesting.

After lunch at a greasy taco dive, where I picked at the lettuce in a tostada, we finally arrived at the venue for sound check. The Melting Pot, a quaint coffee shop that hosted local bands, offered a stark contrast to Sunset Boulevard's House of Blues the night before. During the sound check, I pulled out an empty fold-out chair at the back of the room. As I waited, I felt someone's eyes on me and turned around to see a guy I recognized from church. I gave a polite wave.

'Hey, what are you doing all the way out here?' he asked.

'My friend Tanya brought me to see the Eternals. How 'bout you?'

'Oh… uh… I'm performing tonight,' he said as he scooted his chair closer.

I wouldn't have pegged him for a rapper. With his vintage trousers, aqua button-down, and wavy brown hair combed into a mini-pompadour, he had a 1950s swagger about him. He looked more like he would sing doo-wop.

'Oh, cool. What was your name again? Remembering names was never my forte.'

'I'm John… It's Harmony, right?' His brown eyes were wide and honest.

'So, I see you've met Pigeon John,' Tanya said, giving John a friendly slap on the shoulder.

The three of us took a walk to the corner market for a soda. It was dusk; his favorite time of day, he said. And it really was beautiful. The air was soft and still warm from the day. Burnt orange slivers of light peeked through an indigo sky. Haphazard 20-somethings scooted along the street, wearing flip-flops and board shorts. I was starting to feel better.

'What are you into?' John asked.

'Into? You mean, like, what do I do?'

'I mean "What are you into?" You know: do you like bookstores, coffee shops, going to the movies; that sort of thing?'

That's a new one, I thought. I was thankful he wasn't asking me what I did for a living. I didn't feel like lying to him; but I didn't know how to answer. What *am* I into? I thought to myself.

'I like to dance.' It was the only thing I could think of. The only thing I still had left. Everything else I was 'into' revolved around Derrick. I did what he did. I liked what he liked. I ate what he ate. It took too much effort to want what *I* wanted. It was so much easier to want what *he* wanted; to become who he wanted.

That night, Brainwash Projects and The Eternals performed for a room full of sweaty hipsters and surfer types. Rhyming over thick, gritty beats, they spat witty humor about dating cheerleaders and splendid girls in little shirts. B-boys and B-girls in hats and Pumas mouthed the lyrics. Besides being good, they were funny. During the show, I laughed as much as I danced. A cheering room sent them off stage, and a middle-aged man in a heavily worn plaid shirt and jeans stood up and took a mic from the stand. His sandy hair was scruffy, but clean.

'Bird asked me to come up here and share my story with you,' he began, and the bustling group fell into a respectful hush. The quiet sound of percolating coffee permeated the room.

'I used to be pretty jacked up. Running the streets; using; the whole nine…' He paced leisurely as he spoke. 'My addiction got so bad, I ended up losing everything. I was homeless. And uh… that's what my life was before God. Before I got to know Him.'

One moment, the crowd was head-bobbing; the next, they were listening to this man read a Scripture. A girl wearing a hand-knit Rasta tam reached into her canvas purse and pulled out a small Bible to read along. Tanya listened attentively.

'I am the vine, you are the branches. He who abides in me, and I in him, bears much fruit; for without Me you can do nothing. If anyone does not abide in Me, he is cast out as a branch and is withered. John 15:5–6,' the man read. 'I finally realized that unless I remained in Him, I couldn't bear fruit. I was like the withered branch,' the man continued. Heads throughout the room nodded in agreement with the man's conclusion.

On the ride home I contemplated the night. The Pacific

waters were deep onyx, rippling into the abyss outside my window. I could not tell where the ocean ended and my thoughts began. *OK, God. I have been trying to do this on my own, and look where it has taken me. My very body has become a commodity. I take my clothes off for strangers, and squander my earnings – giving it all away in hopes that I can make him need me enough to want me. I am chasing a man who is too selfish to ever really love me. There is a cold iron fist clenching my heart, and I feel like I am dying.*

I am a withered branch, lying twisted and dry on the side of a riverbank. I can see the water, and I long for it to quench me. But I am distant; separated. Apart from the source that will give me the strong, thick roots I need; roots that burst through rock and ground to get to the nourishing waters.

The man said there is a vine – a tree – that I can be grafted into. I need to be grafted in. What does it mean to abide in You? Show me how. I am tired of being that withered branch, brittle and shriveling.

René's car hummed in the quiet night, and a gentle knowing came to my heart. There was a tie that needed to be severed; a cord keeping me apart from the Source. Somehow, I knew that sex was that chain. Strong and tangled, it seemed to bind all the other ties together, holding me there in that desolate place. Every time I slept with Derrick, I gave him a piece of myself, and withered just a little bit more.

The phone felt heavy in my hand. I hung up and placed it gently on my nightstand, waiting for the breakdown I expected to have. I imagined that I was supposed to throw myself on the bed and cry for hours about losing everything I had hoped for. Only the tears didn't come.

I had been preparing all day: reading every Scripture in the Bible that pertained to the issue. I petitioned God while pacing barefoot on my grey carpet.

'God, if You really want me to do this, then You are going to have to give me the strength.'

When I told Derrick I wanted to stop having sex – that I was going to save myself for marriage – I was prepared to lose him. I had been having sex since the day after my fourteenth birthday; sex was my collateral. It was how I kept men around. I knew exactly what Derrick would say when I called him.

'Then we can't be together any more.'

I was right. After the phone call, I went to the kitchen to wash the dishes. I tiptoed through my living room as if one wrong step would set off a land mine and my world would explode. Still the tears did not come. I filled the basin with warm water and lemon-scented dish soap and started washing. The phone rang again, and a plate slipped out of my hand into the soapy water. I watched it careen to the bottom of the sink and waited for it to break before I answered. It didn't.

It was Derrick again. I couldn't believe he was even calling me. After our last conversation, I wasn't sure if he would ever call again. I was starting to think I didn't want him to.

'You said you didn't want to have sex because I'm not committed to you.' There was a long silence before he spoke again. 'I am ready to commit to you. I'll leave it all behind. The ripping and running. I was getting tired of it, anyway.'

I could swear the wind stopped blowing, and even the ficus tree outside my window was still and quiet. Not a leaf was rustling.

'You realize I am not going to have sex until I'm married?' I said this calm and steady.

'I'll wait…'

My mouth went dry.

'I want to marry you, Harmony.' I am pretty certain I could hear sincerity in his voice.

For a moment, I felt I was in one of those dreams where you try to speak, but you can't. The words were trapped in the back of my throat. I thought I had prepared myself for every possible outcome. Whether it was arguing, convincing, silence, or absence, I was ready for anything. Anything but this, the very thing I had always thought I wanted.

'OK. So what does that mean?' My words were slow and staccato.

'I want to be with you. You are the one I want to end up with. That has always been the plan.' This was the first I had heard of any sort of plan.

'OK. So this means we're official. No more Gina; no more other girls? Just us?' I sat down on my couch and pondered the blue Picasso print on my wall. The woman depicted was naked and crouched into a ball. Her back was turned, and her face tucked into the crook of her arm. I felt as though I was right there with her, in that somber space.

'I'm done running around with those other girls… Listen, I'm on my way over. We can talk then.'

I walked to my bedroom and fell face down onto my mattress. Tears slipped quietly down my cheeks. I lay there until the comforter beneath my cheek was wet and itchy. Then I began to wail: a deep, guttural cry that caused my chest to heave. I rolled into a fetal position and moaned like a grieving woman. Isn't this what I had always wanted? Isn't this what I had been fighting for all those years? Wasn't this the thing that I thought was going to fill the gaping hole inside me? If this was the fix I had been chasing after, then why didn't I feel complete?

A quiet and tender voice replied to my heart; it wrapped itself around me like a soft, worn quilt.

'Precious daughter, he was never meant to fill you. He was never what you were looking for. I am here with you. I will never leave you. You will never have to strive for my love; it is undying. I am who you have been searching for.'

That afternoon, I had been given everything I thought I needed, and it still wasn't enough. I cried first in despair, then in surrender. Relinquishing all of my needs and cares to Him, a quiet peace permeated my being and began to fill the aching void inside me. There was a stillness in my heart, and I lay there until I dozed off to sleep.

When I heard the doorknob turn, I was jolted from a quiet sleep. My legs were thick with reluctance as I walked to the next room to greet him. Derrick was grinning, revealing a dimple on his cheek I rarely saw. He seemed happy. I wasn't. This wasn't how I expected it to go. His expression changed the moment he looked at my face.

'Derrick, we have to talk.'

He sat down next to me.

'I can't do this. I don't think this is going to work,' I continued.

'What's not going to work?' He seemed baffled. I couldn't bring myself to answer.

'What?' he demanded, looking angrier than I had anticipated. His face twisted into a grimace.

'I don't think we should be together.' I wasn't ready to let him go completely, so I offered him a consolation package. 'We can still be friends and hang out… and don't worry, I'll still help you out and everything…'

He got up and headed for the door.

'Wait! Derrick, come back here so we can talk…' I called out after him.

'There's nothing to talk about.' He slammed the door so hard Picasso's *Blue Woman* was knocked askew. I flung the door open and went after him, not because I needed him to stay, but because I had become so accustomed to chasing him. I was a bystander in my own life as old habits took over.

'Derrick, wait. Please wait, so we can talk.' He was walking so fast I could hardly keep up with him. I was panting and crying and becoming hysterical, in my effort to stop him.

I reached out to try to grab his hand. He whipped around, grabbed me by the shoulders and shoved me back hard. I stumbled, trying not to hit the ground, and grabbed a chain-link fence to keep from hitting the concrete. When I regained my balance, I stood there in the middle of the sidewalk and watched him walk away. My heart was beating fast and frantic. My lungs burned with each breath coursing through them. The one thing I longed for had come and gone. I found myself going through the motions of running after him, but in my heart the issue was settling.

It was time to start running toward a greater Love. As I walked back home, He whispered my name in the afternoon sun that shone gentle and warm. Each ray was a reminder of His kindness outstretched towards my weary soul.

I stared at the wall-to-wall mural of an orange beach sunset scene as I waited for Tony in the owner's, Sal's, 'office'. It was so like Sal to have such a spectacle on his wall. The mural looked as if it belonged on a cheesy postcard you'd buy on the Boardwalk. The first time I met Sal, he tried to hypnotize me so I would have sex with him, and then took me off the schedule until I agreed to go to dinner with him. I didn't sleep with him, but I did relent and join him for dinner, so that I could keep my job. I managed to cop such a horrible attitude with him that by the end of the night, he told me that I was a perfect example of why he preferred Asian girls. Women like me were too 'mouthy'. And the Asian girls he referred to were the ones he met during his sex-tourism trips to Thailand, where he indulged in his pick of teenage sex slaves.

Now Tony walked into Sal's office, and I shifted on the scratchy, polyester sectional sofa.

'So what's going on, Monique?' Tony asked, as he sat on the matching love-seat opposite me.

'He wasn't tipping. How can a man sit at the stage like that and not even have the decency to tip a dollar?!' I complained.

'You can't go around knocking drinks on customers.' He was half-hearted in his reprimand. I could tell he empathized with me.

'I made it look like an accident,' I said, smiling sheepishly.

'You can't keep doing that, Monique.'

I could hear the distant thump of music coming from the club.

'I don't want to do any of this any more,' I said, folding my arms and slumping in my seat. 'I am so tired of this. I just don't know how long I can take it. I try to get out there to make money, but I just want to punch someone,' I ranted.

'Believe me, I know.' Tony leaned in and rested his arms on his knees. 'I've been in this business for 20 years and have wanted to get out almost as long. Guy like me, working here all these years, it's hard to get out there and get a regular job. Believe me, I've tried.' Tony sat back and stared off at the painted ocean on the wall.

Twenty years before, wanting to escape his ties to an organized crime ring, Tony checked himself into a motel with enough drugs to kill himself and a handgun to finish the job. Sufficiently high, Tony was working up the nerve to put a bullet in his head with a game of Russian roulette when he heard a knock at his motel door. It was a high-school buddy he hadn't seen in years. Tony hadn't told anyone that he had checked into that motel, so he grilled the guy about how he had found him.

'God told me you were here, and I know what you are about to do.'

This was just wild enough to get Tony's attention, so he obliged his old buddy's request to go out for a beer. At the end of the night, the guy led Tony to Christ, right there in the bar's parking lot. Tony didn't kill himself. Instead, he started looking for legitimate work. The next day, a man on the street came up and offered Tony a gig as a bouncer in a club. Turned out it was a strip club.

After a few moments, Tony broke his trance, reached over and pulled out his briefcase from beside the couch.

'I want to show you something,' he said, pulling an envelope out from the case. 'You remember Amanda?'

'Oh, yeah, I remember her.' She was hard to forget. Six feet tall, without her heels.

'She sent me this.' He went on to read an excerpt from the letter. '"Dear Tony, thank you for talking to me that night. You reminded me that the life inside of me was precious and helped me make a good decision. If it weren't for you, I might not have my baby girl."' He held up a picture of Amanda holding a little baby girl with wispy brown hair. 'She was going to have an abortion. She came to me.' Tony pinched the bridge of his nose and squinted his eyes. He was holding back tears. 'I want out, but sometimes I wonder if God has me here for a reason; if He wants me here in the trenches to help girls like Amanda.' He shook his head and looked me in the eye. 'Monique, you want out of here?'

'Yes, I really do, Tony.'

'Then do you mind if I pray with you?'

Nobody had ever prayed with me before. I wasn't sure what to do. Should I stand up? Kneel down? Tony reached over to his briefcase and opened it again. Inside was the gun he always carried, and beside it a small brown vial. He took out the vial and showed it to me; it looked like the kind of thing people use for carrying cocaine. He stood up, and I followed his lead.

'This is... uhhh... anointing oil,' Tony stuttered. 'Um... do you mind if I use some when I pray with you?'

'Sure.' I had nothing to lose.

Tony dabbed the oil with his middle finger and touched the oil to my forehead. As I stood there, half-naked in my stilettos in the back room of a strip club, Tony prayed for me. I started to think that God was bigger than I had given Him credit for. That He was the kind of God who shows up at strip clubs and seeks after guys like Tony; after girls like me.

My grandmother held a cup of black coffee in the palms of her hands and we both gazed out of the window of the breakfast nook at my father's house in a suburb outside of Seattle, Washington. Before us was a garden atop a cliff, filled with flowers and bird feeders to attract the wildest and most beautiful birds. Below was the Pacific Ocean, its slate-grey waters whipping and smashing onto the rocks below. Neither of us was looking at any of this. We were both watching my father.

He was sitting on a lawn chair, wearing a navy-blue bathrobe over his beige velour sweatsuit. He held his cigarette between his index finger and thumb like a joint, and drew in one last puff, before smashing it down into a hand-painted ashtray his wife had no doubt picked out. His neck jet forward, as he lifted a brimming glass of Scotch on the rocks to his lips, careful not to spill a drop. I contemplated going out and sitting with him, but I still hadn't come up with anything to say, other than 'Good morning'.

'You can't know how hard it is as a mother. I just don't understand why he doesn't want a relationship with me,' she lamented, as she blew on her steamy beverage.

'Imagine being his daughter,' I piped up. We had had

the same conversation dozens of times before and still hadn't resolved whose pain was the greater.

'Why do you suppose he brought us out here to visit after all these years? Do you think she finally said something?' My grandmother's bright blue eyes were wanting and searching. The *she* who she was referring to was Christy, my father's current wife. Five years before, during what was supposed to be a cherished holiday weekend when more than five of my family members were actually under one roof, my father brought her to meet the family. We barely made it through Thanksgiving dinner when personalities clashed to such an extent that my father and his bride-to-be checked into a hotel and never came back. His fiancée gave him an ultimatum: us or her. He chose her, and we hadn't seen him since.

They had just moved to this house in Washington, and it seemed his wife was lonely and depressed enough in the dismal Seattle weather that she just might have had a change of heart. As for my father, not much had changed. I reached for the bottle of expensive perfume sitting on the kitchen table and sprayed it on myself for the second time that morning. My father had bought my grandmother and me a bottle each the day before, during an afternoon trip to a fancy department store with a live pianist playing elevator music. When my father handed his credit card to the salesperson, I imagined I was the kind of daughter that could get her father to spring for all kinds of fancy purchases in upscale department stores. For a moment, I was 'Daddy's little girl'.

'Let me have summa that. I left mine upstairs,' my grandmother said in her East Texan accent, as she reached for my bottle of perfume. 'Now wasn't that nice of him, to buy those for us? He didn't have to do that, you know.' She wanted to make sure he got the credit due for this act of kindness. It brought him one step closer to being the kind of son she dreamed of. I opened the sliding glass door, and chilling ocean air lashed at my face.

'Well if you're going out there, I'll probably join you in a minute.' My grandmother couldn't stand to miss out on any conversations.

I sat on a lawn chair next to my father, and wrapped my arms tightly around my own waist to keep warm. I still didn't have a plan. I just figured I would insert myself into his world to see what would happen.

'Chilly, chilly, chilly...' This was his attempt at starting conversation. It was his way of talking without really having anything to say. He did the same thing on long car rides, by reading random billboard signs aloud to fill the silence.

'Yep; it's cold out here,' I replied. At least he was trying. A hummingbird flittered about, examining a bird feeder filled with bright red nectar.

'So, Christy really likes birdwatching? She showed me her binoculars and that bird book.' I wish I could have come up with something better than that.

'Yep; she likes birds. She's a birdwatcher.' He was habitually shaking his right foot at the ankle.

The sliding glass door opened behind us, and my grandmother walked out of the house. She had gone upstairs to get her coat, a multi-colored tweed with loose, feathery loops of fabric.

'Well, good mornin',' she said as she made her grand entrance.

My father sat up and tightened his bathrobe. 'Good morning, Mother. Well, I should go take a shower,' he said, as he stood up and headed back into the house.

My grandmother and I sat there quietly after he left. I wished I had something more captivating to say; something that would have held him there next to me. I felt a longing to say or do or *be* something that would make him realize that I was worth loving and having around. It was the same way I had always felt about Derrick. Only where my father was absent, at least Derrick had been present.

There was a deep wound in my heart, a longing for my father's approval. And it wasn't that he disapproved of me. He had never said anything that would lead me to believe that; but the pain was in all of the things he never said. In Derrick I had found someone who would at least cast an opinion of me, even if it was a negative one. The fact that he even took the time getting to know me to form an opinion had been enough for me.

I wondered who I would have been if my father hadn't left my mother and me. Who would I be if I lived here on this bluff, overlooking the Puget Sound, I wondered, and I noticed the way a tiny yellow flower hung sideways over the edge of its clay pot, striving to find a grey sliver of sunlight in the cold Seattle sky. I was tired of striving and reaching for their approval. A gentle, loving voice in my heart was telling me I didn't have to.

'Well, just look at that, Harmony,' my grandmother said, pointing to the hummingbird as it sipped on artificial nectar. I could hear the vibrating sound of its tiny wings flapping in the air. Just then, it zipped away from the bird feeder to the garden, where it landed on a hibiscus flower and discovered its satiating sweetness.

Why would the hummingbird keep going to that man-made feeder when there was a garden set before it, filled with the real thing? I contemplated this, and it occurred to me that I had been doing the same.

Twenty-Two

The night was falling blue and grey over Inglewood, California. In the distance, the city lights cast an orange tint on the thick layer of smog. I took a different route: the back way; trying to avoid the tourists and businessmen fighting their way down the 405 Freeway, driving zero miles an hour to LAX.

The sound of Kirk Franklin & The Family filled the Alpine speakers in my Honda Civic: 'Silver and gold, silver and gold; I'd rather have Jesus than silver and gold.' The music comforted me, and I began to sing along, not realizing the weight of my words. I wore the same ankle-length, green sundress with tiny white flowers I always wore. No panties; no bra. That way, I wouldn't have lines on my skin from the elastic and wire of undergarments. The truth is, it didn't matter what I was wearing. It never did. It all came off, anyway. I don't want to be here; this is not where I want to be, I thought to myself, as I pulled up to the club.

I noticed the sign. I had always hated it. I had told the owner, Sal, to change it, but he never listened to me. The 1970s-style faded orange and red letters hung limply: 'Live Live Nude Nudes' – as if there could be dead nudes inside. I suppose it's possible. Within moments, I would be in that place, stripped down to nothing, feeling very much like a dead nude. One time an *e* fell off and the sign said 'Live Live Nude Nud s'. It took Sal months to change it.

A large man with weathered black skin and ashy calloused hands greeted me on the way into the club. I smiled. He tried to smile. He was missing more teeth than he had left. We chatted on our way to the door… pretending to care about the weather and how empty or full the parking lot was.

Elvia was sitting outside, smoking a cigarette. Her jet-black, stringy hair matched her eyes, a stark contrast from her pale, pasty skin. She wore nothing but a bra and panties, with nine-inch, patent-leather stilettos, still she looked Gothic. Her collagen-filled, deep burgundy lips parted into a slick smile as I passed. The club smelled of cigarettes, Victoria's Secret body spray and greasy French fries. It always seemed to me an unlikely combination. Strippers and cheeseburgers.

At the DJ booth, Doug the one-line-wonder had his grinning mouth pressed against the microphone.

'Upon the main stage, the lovely young lady… Jaaaade,' he oozed. 'Monique, what will it be tonight? A little Erykah Badu?'

'No, Rickie,' I said, smiling tolerantly as he looked me up and down.

The locker room was busy with girls changing shifts. I pulled out a towel and placed it on the floor in front of the full-length mirror. Straddling my legs across the wall to stretch my limbs, I began to paint my face; paint my mask. It was one of the ways I created distance: from customers, from myself.

MAC powder: C3, a warm golden hue. A soft brown shadow to fill in my pale blonde eyebrows. Eyebrows frame your face, and shaping them is an art form, really. Grace taught me that. She told me to study the faces of porcelain dolls; how their brows arch and curve so delicately. It was Jade who showed me how to apply liquid liner with a steady hand. A thin line of black painted carefully just above the lashes to accent my light green eyes. Finishing touch: a deep red lip-stick.

'For God's sake, do something with your hair, Monique!' Summer cackled.

I ignored her. Even if I did know how to use a blow dryer, why on earth would I waste 45 minutes fussing with my hair, when I could make $1,000 a night without looking as if I had just stepped out of a salon? Warm and limber, I headed towards the tiny bathroom behind the main stage. As all 'totally nude' strippers do, I ever so glamorously bent over in front of the mirror to check for toilet paper. All clear.

In the bathroom stall, Kristin was bent over too. Her finger was in her throat and she was vomiting. I suppose she didn't want to dance on a full stomach.

Angel emerged from the main stage curtain with her long thin silky blonde hair covering her face – covering her depression. She always reminded me of a weeping willow when she danced: swaying around the stage, her wispy hair fluttering limply about. She was headed to the dressing room to cry. She always cried. I used to try to comfort her. 'What's wrong? Do you need to talk?' I would ask. But she would just sit there, with her head hung low, mascara running down her face, and reply, 'No thanks, I'm OK.' As long as I knew her, she was never OK.

While I waited for my cue to enter the stage, I glanced over my shoulder at my reflection in the mirror. My skin was dark gold, tanned to perfection. I noticed that there was more definition in my quads, and my body was long and slender, from all the dance classes I had been taking. I enjoyed a small but ever-fleeting feeling of confidence. *You will never be enough*, a seething voice whispered in my head.

'Upon the main stage, the lovely young lady... Monique,' Doug gushed.

Rickie Lee Jones's 'Chuck E's in Love' began to play. Her music was the soundtrack to my life, comforting and familiar. I bounced and bobbed around the stage in a flirty little dress for the first song: twirling around the poles and climbing them in displays of strength and expertise. All of this is one big effort to make art – or, at least, something more meaningful than what it really was.

Exit. Then enter nude. This time, creeping and slinking to

Rickie's 'Coolsville'. Don't they hear the sorrow and pain in her voice? Don't they see the sorrow and pain in me? I thought to myself. They can't see me. They will never see me. I am naked before them, and they will never see. I was both saddened and relieved by this thought.

'It's OK. It's not that bad. It's OK. It's not that bad,' Rickie crooned, over and over again… trying to convince herself, just as I was. It *was* that bad. For both of us… in that song, in that moment. It always had been. My hurt was deep and hidden, behind a straight-A student with a California smile. I could feel an ever-present, crushing heaviness around my heart, like iron, restricting flow and freedom.

The iron was Derrick. He had me in his grip, and I couldn't break free. When he realized he couldn't pay his bills without me, he took me up on my offer to stay friends. I could tell by the way he looked at me that it hurt his ego to do this. I wanted to say 'No', but I didn't know how. I didn't know how to let him go. How does the ravenous lion stop chasing the gazelle when it knows no other way to survive? I realized I needed to stop the hunt, even though it seemed to go against my very instinct. I was tired of pursuing, and giving and sacrificing… in exchange for what? Constant unfaithfulness, belittling, and degradation? A baby by another woman? The responsibility to support him and his baby, and his baby's mama, and to fund his ridiculous hobby? Who spends tens of thousands of dollars on turning a low-budget Honda into a blinged-out race car? I am being pimped. And, yes, it is that bad! I thought to myself.

A man placed a dollar at my feet. An unusual feeling of nervousness swept over me. It was the feeling you have in one of those dreams where you are in high school and you realize you forgot to get dressed. You scramble around in vain, looking for something to cover you. It's too late… you have already been exposed. Suddenly, I felt naked! Stripped. It took everything in me to keep from running off the stage before the song ended. That is when I noticed them; all of the men staring intensely. They were gawking and leering; consuming me with their eyes. An overweight man with glasses and a pink, smirking face leaned in and placed a $10 bill on the brass rail that surrounded the stage. A man in a white dress shirt sipped his drink. His eyes were beady and black, empty and stealing.

These men saw all of me. They knew nothing of me, but they saw all of me. My dress was backstage, and there was nothing to cover me. Nothing to hide behind. When the song ended, I bolted to the locker room, where I opened my locker and stood there, gazing at the array of lotions and body sprays like a person looking into a refrigerator and wondering what they should have to eat. What do I want? I asked myself.

I took a deep breath, trying to shake the foreboding feeling. My eyes landed on the sticker I had placed inside of my locker to motivate me: 'Let's make $$$!!!' I can't quit now, I told myself and God. Besides, Derrick wouldn't hear of it. 'It's just not smart,' he would say. Nothing I ever did was smart.

I slipped on my little plaid red dress and black heels, dabbed the perspiration from my forehead and hit the floor. Gliding across the room to the bar, I looked intently at all the customers as a cheetah would her prey. Inhale.

Just as I approached a small, sturdy little man from behind, the Prince song 'Purple Rain' filled the room, and my heart skipped a beat. I flashed back to the memory of me as an awkward 19-year-old girl who, thinking she had no options, decided to work as an exotic dancer for two months. I pictured myself, stripping off my little cotton dress and clomping around the stage in my street shoes. Dizzy with nervousness, I kept my balance by clutching the brass poles along the stage.

This memory stopped me in my tracks. Three years later, I was still in the same place, doing the same thing, hoping things would change. How *could* I quit? It was a vicious cycle. The more money I made, the more I gave to Derrick. The more money I gave him, the more he needed me. The more he needed me, the less likely he was to leave me... the less likely I was to have to be alone. Even though I had stopped sleeping with him, I still hadn't managed to let him go completely. The loneliness would be unbearable, I told myself. Besides, I would only replace Derrick with some other guy who would treat me just as poorly, if not worse. I preferred familiar dysfunction to the unfamiliar. At least I knew what to expect each day.

The man in front of me was transfixed by the woman on the stage and didn't notice me, standing there behind him. He would never know that I was prepared to lead him into the little red booth, where I would strip down and take off all my clothes in exchange for a few crumpled-up bills. The song enveloped me like a lavender ribbon, wrapping itself around my entire body. I became caught up: by the song; by the moment.

I am in this moment. Here. Now. And in that moment, I became aware: aware of my ivory bones, and the muscles and tendons wrapped around them; of the blood coursing through my veins; of my heart, beating hard in my chest.

Standing on thin, worn carpet, I wobbled slightly on my stilettos. I had paced and strutted across that floor on hundreds of nights before. I began to realize that I had participated in the wearing of the carpet. I had participated in so much more wearing than my mind could comprehend. Slowly, I placed one foot behind the other, until I stood at the back of the club. The room seemed to expand and contract all at once. Prince was still singing about purple rain. He was empathizing with me.

'Honey, I know, I know, I know times are changing. It's time we all reach out for something new. That means you too,' he snarled. There was a slide show in my mind: Derrick – me – Gina – the baby – the money – me – God – me – the money – Derrick – that car! – the bills – me – Derrick – God.

And there is God. And He is here. Suddenly, I saw. I saw Nicole in the table-dance booth, swinging her leg over a customer's head and propping it up on the rail to give him a better view. Her eyes danced around the room. *She is disengaged. She is naked.*

The girl on stage was bent over on all fours and glancing over her shoulder sheepishly at a man in a suit. *She is naked. We are all naked here.*

'I can't quit now!' I pleaded silently with God, and myself, and anyone who would listen.

That is when I heard. A small and still voice whispered to the core of my heart and being.

'I am here. I am with you. I will never leave you.'

Exhale. *He is here. He is with me. He will never leave me. I will never be alone. This is truth.* And somehow my ivory bones and my tendons and blood were in harmony as truth resonated throughout my body. *Yes, I am caught up; in truth; in Him.*

I began to rise. I was already standing, but I began to rise. I lifted my head and eyes as I walked directly over to my manager, Gabe, with his kind, freckled face.

'I'm leaving.' The words formed awkwardly in my mouth. It was almost a question.

'For the night?' he asked.

'For ever,' I replied.

Leaving Gabe dumbfounded and wondering, I walked briskly towards the locker room to pack up my things. Elvia stopped me in the hallway. 'What's wrong? What's going on?' she asked.

'That's it. I am leaving. I can't take this any more. I have to get out of here,' I rattled off.

She grabbed me by the shoulders and looked directly into my eyes. In a calm and sedating voice, she spoke. 'No, Monique. Just go home, get some rest, and come back tomorrow.'

I pulled away from her grip. 'No, I am quitting,' I affirmed with a growing confidence.

In the locker room I announced that all my clothes were for sale. Though confused, the other girls began making offers. Chloe, a slender blonde who spent her days at the beach flirting with surfer boys, had always wanted my long, sheer black dress: $20; gone. Grace, with her bright red, silicone lips and neatly painted eyebrows, grabbed for my slinky little Marilyn Monroe number: $20; gone.

One by one, I got rid of each article of clothing, and with it a piece of Monique, the identity I created and sold: the woman I dressed up as and pretended to be. *Harmony; I am Harmony*, I thought to myself. *I am Harmony, and I am leaving.*

But first, there was a call that had to be made. I climbed into the payphone booth behind the dressing rooms, shut the door and dialed the number. With my ear pressed firmly against the phone, I could hear my heart beating between the rings.

'Hello?'

'Hey, it's me…' My voice was shaky and soft.

'What's up?' he asked impatiently.

'Ummm. I have to tell you something…'

'Yeees?'

I could almost see him, sitting there on his fake leather couch, gesturing with his hand for me to hurry up and stop taking so long to say what I had to say. I could practically hear him rolling his eyes, frustrated that I was wasting precious time that could be spent playing video games or watching basketball.

'Helloooo? Aren't you supposed to be working?' he chimed.

'That's actually what I am calling about. I quit.'

'You what??'

'I just can't do this any more.'

Silence.

'Derrick... are you still there?'

'Yeah, I'm here. Well, it looks like you have made up your mind, then…'

Silence.

'Is that it?' That meant he was done talking.

'Yes.'

'A'ight, then.' And with that he hung up.

I sat and contemplated our call. The Harmony he knew would hardly take a trip to the grocery store without consulting him first. He was probably calculating and strategizing and trying to figure out how on earth he was losing his grip on me. Even I couldn't fully grasp it. I only knew that I was falling in love, and into the hands of someone greater than Derrick and me and the life I had been living. I went back to the dressing room to collect what was left of my clothes and to say goodbye to the other girls.

'You'll be back; everyone comes back,' Summer said casually, while scrunching her curly brown hair into perfect locks. She didn't even turn around to look at me.

My mother had said something similar when I told her I had found an apartment the month before my eighteenth birthday. Neither one of them knew that these comments only served to strengthen my resolve. I would not be back.

Driving down Century Boulevard, I felt something that reminded me of when I was a child, barefoot and running through the sand at top speed, straight towards the crashing waves of the ocean. The deep and vast and wonderful ocean, where I would throw my entire body into the crest of the waves before they broke. It was a feeling of abandon that can only happen when safe and free.

There was a lifting and a releasing. I could have been worried that I would lose Derrick for good; that he would leave me for a woman with more means. I could have been worried that my pesky little savings wouldn't even cover one month of the bills I had accumulated between the apartments and the cars and all that I had in my name. I could have been worried about those things, but I wasn't. Instead, I found myself going top speed towards the crest of something deep and vast and wonderful.

But for Charles, there was nothing about the club I hadn't gladly left behind. I pictured him alone in his big dusty house, tucked high on a hillside filled with haunting remnants of what was once a full life. A piano that his deceased wife would no longer play; a kitchen she would never again cook in; an office with no work to be done. I felt sorry that I was leaving him, and I asked God to bring him company, or to do something – *anything* – to make it better. I needed to put my past behind me, and that included Charles. Sorrowfully, I picked up the phone to break the news that I would no longer be working at the strip club, and no, we wouldn't be able to see each other socially. When a woman's voice answered the phone, I became hopeful that my prayers had been answered. *Maybe his niece is in town*. He was only able to see her once a year, but he was wild about her. But her tone made it clear. All was not well in his big, dusty home.

'He's not here.'

'Oh. Well, can you tell him Monique called?' He was the only customer I had ever told my real name, but he was too senile to remember it.

I questioned whether or not I should even leave a message. If it was his niece, what was I supposed to say? 'Oh, by the way, your uncle goes to strip clubs three times a week, and I am his favorite stripper'?

'Monique?' she said knowingly. 'This is the other Monique. He would want to see you.' She was the Monique that preceded me; the one whom Charles saw regularly until she left the club to build a career in soft porn. I wondered what she was doing at his house. The last I heard, she had been living in another state.

'What do you mean, he would want to see me?'

'He's in the hospital. You didn't know?'

'Oh my gosh! Is he OK?'

'He had a heart attack. He was in critical condition, but he seems to be recovering now.'

As I wrote down the visiting hours and directions to the hospital, tears tumbled down my cheeks. I worried for his heart – for his weak and failing heart – and how it would hurt even more when I walked out of his life.

The night I left the club, I made a commitment to myself that I would never return to that life. And as much as I wished that we had met on a park bench or some other innocent, benign place, Charles was a part of that life. He was the only one I would call. I felt I owed him that: a goodbye, proper closure.

Even as I drove, lost, up and down narrow residential streets in San Pedro, looking for the hospital, I wondered if I was doing the right thing by going to see him in person. I looked at the passenger seat – at the large, green, leather-bound study Bible my aunt bought me – as if for directions. I had been reading it just about every waking moment, consuming the words, letting them fill me. It didn't all make sense, and some of it seemed flat-out crazy, especially the parts about wars and giants; but even that added to the mystery of it all. There was some big history and truth and eternity that existed outside me, yet I had become a part of it. I wanted to know all about it.

I saw a large white stone statue of Mary, with her arms outstretched, before I saw the hospital. When your faith is new – before it gets trampled on by time and complacency – everything is wondrous, no detail too insignificant for reflection. Even the simple fact that Charles had ended up in this particular hospital, with a statue of Mary out front, seemed to validate the very existence of God. I walked up the steps to the entrance and came upon the reception desk.

'How can I help you?' a round Filipino woman greeted me.

'I am here to see Charles Collins.'

'May I have your name?'

I stammered a bit. If I said that my name was Harmony and they went to tell Charles that 'Harmony' was here to visit him, I'd run the risk of him saying that he had never met a 'Harmony'. If I told the receptionist that my name was Monique, the receptionist might ask for ID and find out that I was lying.

'Harmony. Harmony Huhn.'

'What is your relation?' she asked, as she scanned her log for his name.

I hadn't thought about that. What was I supposed to tell this woman?

'I'm a friend of his.'

The woman looked up from her roster inquisitively. 'His friend?' she repeated. I suppose that she was expecting to hear something more along the lines of 'granddaughter'.

'Yes. I'm a friend of his.'

'Is he expecting you?' she asked.

'His niece said that he wanted to see me,' I lied.

'Let me see if he is able to have visitors at this time.'

The receptionist placed a brief call, before addressing me again.

'All right; he was just moved from ICU; he is in Room 411.'

As I approached his room, I heard another voice there, and wondered if I should keep walking. What if a family member was visiting? I had no business showing my face in there.

'OK, eat up, Mr Collins,' I heard the voice say, and then a petite young nurse with silky brown hair walked out of the room.

I released my bated breath. 'Is he OK?' I asked, hoping that she was as friendly as she seemed.

'Oh,' she said, seemingly startled to see me. 'Mr Collins, it looks like you have a visitor,' she said in the kind of soft feminine voice you use when speaking to children and seniors. I followed her back into the room and stopped at the end of the small entryway.

'You're doing much better now, aren't you, Mr Collins?'

'Yes, I am.' His voice was scratchy and creaky.

'You have a visitor,' she noted.

I turned the corner, to see him in his hospital bed looking frail and old. He was wearing a thin, blue hospital gown that fell on one side, exposing his bony shoulder. His white hair stood on end in places, like cotton wire, and his drooping cheeks seemed to pull at his face so it was an inch longer than before. As he registered who I was, he began to smile.

'Well, hello there!' he said, in the jolliest voice he could muster.

'Hi, Charles. I called your house and "the other" Monique told me you were here. I've been worried about you…'

'I'm doing much better now. They moved me out of ICU last night.'

I stood at the foot of his bed, clutching my Bible and purse, unsure of whether I should sit or stand. 'You gave me quite a scare there, Charles. I am so happy to know that you are OK. How long are they going to keep you here?'

'Well, I just don't know…'

'I hope they're taking good care of you in here.' I used a playful, motherly voice.

'Yep. They're taking pretty good care of me,' he said, wearing a boyish grin.

I looked around the room and saw a fold-out chair against the wall. 'May I?'

'Certainly. Have a seat.'

The room went silent as our banter lost its momentum.

I pulled the chair to the side of his bed and lowered myself into it. He would live, and I was relieved, but there was an ending to it all, and it fell heavy upon us. I lifted my eyes to meet his gaze. He held me there, tears forming in both of our eyes.

'Charles… I quit. I'm not working there any more.'

He knit his brow, and a welling tear took a plunge over the edge of his lower lid and fell down his cheek, crashing on the white hospital sheet. He forced a smile as true as he could.

'Good for you, honey. I know that you were tired of that place.'

'I just can't do it any more, Charles.' I was clearly speaking about the line of work, but subtly referring to all that went along with it, including him. If I was really going to leave my old life behind me, I had to leave it *all* behind.

'I know,' he said, in a soft and tender voice. 'I know.'

'Thank you.' It was the only response that fit.

'Charles, do you ever think about God?' The words tumbled out of my mouth.

'Yes, honey, yes I do.' He lowered his head and tears slid down his wrinkled cheeks.

Silence filled the room as I searched for words. How could I describe what I had found? How could I ever do it justice? He looked so frail and alone. And soon, the other Monique would leave, and his empty home would surround him like a museum with artifacts that spoke of days more fulfilling than the ones he would live out. What did I have to offer him, anyhow? What we shared was so far from the way true friendship and intimacy works. He paid me for my time. He paid me to listen to him repeat stories about the moments in his life that were worth an account. He paid me to help him feel as though his life still meant something; that someone still cared for him. And I did. But, for my own sanity and sense of self, I couldn't participate in relationships that had been founded on fantasy and financial transactions any longer.

As everything I thought I was and everything that I allowed to define me had been stripped away, it came to this: love, hope, and faith. These were things worth sharing. And as I looked for ways to comfort Charles, they were all I had to offer.

I worried that Charles would think I was crazy. I worried that the words would come out wrong. What would my mom and Daddy Russ and my brother Noah think, if they could see me here now with this big green Bible? Certainly they would think I had gone mad; that I had become one of those kooky, crusading Christians.

I sat at the edge of Charles's hospital bed and considered risking rejection of the very things I had come to hold closest to my heart. I wanted to share the discovery of a relationship that had touched me at the core of my being. I wanted him to meet the Love of my life. I said the only thing I knew to say.

'Have you ever asked Jesus into your heart?' My voice was soft and shaky.

'Well, I went to Catholic school as a boy, but I just don't know…' his words lingered in the air, and he pulled his hand to his forehead to cover his face. His chest began to rise and fall rhythmically, as sobbing overtook him.

'If you want to, I can pray with you,' I said, nervously pulling at the soft, satiny string that bookmarked the Bible sitting in my lap. I have heard that the most common fear is that of public speaking. I would like to submit that fear of public praying is an overlooked and far more terrifying thing, especially when you have never done it before.

He sucked in a long breath of air and let out a sigh, before he looked up at me. 'I would like that. I would like that very much.'

I pulled my chair closer to him and placed my hand gently on his. I could feel his plump veins underneath my fingertips.

I stammered for words. 'God, thank You for my friend Charles. I pray that… that You would take care of him… and help his heart heal. And God… I pray that You would show him how much You love him, and that he would open his heart to You and that You would comfort him. Tonight while he sleeps, please let him know that… that he isn't alone.'

'Charles, you can say this prayer with me.' Charles's words echoed mine, as he repeated after me.

'God, I want a relationship with You. I ask that You come into my heart and forgive me for every time I have fallen short. Thank You for your forgiveness and for Your love. Thank You that I am new. In Jesus' name, Amen.'

I sat quietly, holding his hand. Even in that aged body of his, there was something so childish and vulnerable about the way he cried. It seemed as though he cried for every time he fell off his bike and hurt his knee, and the time he was shipped off to war, and the time his own wife forgot his name and looked at him as one would at a stranger in her home, and for every night he spent wishing that though she no longer knew him, her warm body was still next to him, soothing him.

When we finally said goodbye, there was finality to it.

I looked at him; he looked at me; we said the words, but the moment seemed so much bigger than our words.

Part of me felt selfish. After all he had done for me, I was leaving him there in a hospital bed. I was walking out of his life. But I knew that I couldn't take care of him. It wasn't my place. I have heard it said that fantasy is a bill of goods. In exchange for money, I gave Charles the fantasy of an intimate friendship. We both wanted to believe the fantasy. In fact, we both *needed* to believe it. He needed a companion and I needed to be someone's companion.

That afternoon, before I left the hospital, I stopped by the nurses' station to speak with the kind nurse I had met in Charles's room.

'Please take good care of him…' I practically begged. 'He's a nice man, and I just want to make sure that he is taken care of.' I tilted my head up to keep the tears from spilling out. 'And please make sure to call me and let me know how he is doing.'

I fished around in my purse, looking for something to write on. My vision blurred, and the tears I had been fighting fell onto my hand. I wrote down my contact information, still trying to hold the sobs in my throat. The nurse assured me that she would keep me in the loop. I left, relieved to know that Charles was in good hands and that he would be OK without me.

I called to check on him at the hospital a few days later, and he told me he had had a stroke the night I left. He expected to recover. But when I called him again, he seemed disoriented, and I wondered if he even knew who I was.

'Charles, it's Monique.' Silence.

'Charles, you remember Monique, don't you?'

'Oh, why yes, of course I do.' But his voice was formal, like a telemarketer.

For the next couple of weeks, I couldn't bring myself to call again, until one morning I sat in my bed and thought of him. I hoped that he had recovered, and that he woke up in the morning with a sense of limitless possibility and promise for his life: that is what I hoped, when I called his house. When he didn't answer, I dialed the hospital.

'Oh yes, hi, I'm looking for Charles Collins, please. I believe he was in Room 411.'

They transferred my call from one place to another, each person who answered telling me that he had been moved from their floor, until finally…

'Who are you looking for?'

'I'm looking for Charles Collins… he was in Room 411 but I think they moved him…'

There was silence on the end of the line.

'Who am I speaking with?' the woman asked.

'I'm a friend of his. You can check his charts; my name is on there. The nurse said she would call me with his progress, but I haven't heard anything from her…'

'I'm sorry. Mr Collins has expired,' she said flatly. My body stiffened.

'He what?'

'He's expired…'

'What do you mean, "expired"?' *Milk expires! People don't expire!*

'He passed away, a couple weeks ago, on November 30th. It looks like he had a stroke… he wasn't able to recover.'

'Why didn't anyone tell me? Someone was supposed to call me…'

'I'm sorry, but the family was notified…'

When I hung up the phone, loss swept over me like a blanket. For a moment, it was the only thing I could feel: a looming sense of absence. I thought it interesting that I hadn't felt it before; that I hadn't somehow known that he and I no longer inhabited the same place together. It felt like betrayal: he was dead and I didn't know it. And what if the nurse had contacted me? I wouldn't have been able to attend his funeral. There would have been too many questions. Who are you? How did you know him? Why didn't he ever talk about you?

Or, worse: what if they knew who I was? What if upon his death the family reviewed his assets, expecting to receive a hefty inheritance, only to find that his savings were gone, his credit cards maxed out and thousands upon thousands of dollars charged to the strip club? It wouldn't take long for them to figure out that he had squandered his money on a stripper. And what would they think of me? What would they think of the tears that I am crying for him?

I was certain to be a shame to the family. I pictured myself attending his funeral, standing unnoticed in the distance at some grassy cemetery, watching through dark shaded glasses as his casket was lowered into the ground. They wouldn't understand that I cared for him. And would they believe that I had set out to live a different life; that I was determined to become the kind of woman that could attend funerals and visit hospitals without fear of disgrace? That even though I was the stripper whom he had spent his life savings on, I was also the girl who had shared the riches of hope and faith with him, wealth that could never be squandered.

I picked up the journal on my nightstand and sat staring at the page. Just what does one write in a moment like this? I thought of my children – the ones I had yet to have – and pictured them sitting in a dusty attic, reading their mother's journal. What would they make of an entry about the death of a customer? Still, it had to be recorded. I couldn't close the book as though it had never happened – as though Charles had never existed. So I wrote:

Charles Collins, died November 30th, found out December 29th.

As I sat waiting for my grandmother's and aunt's flight to arrive, the Los Angeles airport was filled with the quiet, steady hum of commuter traffic. Men and women in tailored suits were contently waiting to get where they were going, while sipping coffee and reading the morning paper. A man with a briefcase whisked by, with his tie slung over his shoulder, going as fast as his feet would carry him without breaking into a run. No one seemed to know what day it was.

Caught up in their sports sections and lattes, nobody noticed my life was changing before their very eyes. It was the morning of my baptism. This wasn't going to be just some ceremony where some preacher man would dunk me in a miniature swimming pool and splash water on my face. It marked the beginning of what would be a new life for me. Everything that had been happening over the past six months, since I first set foot in church, was leading to this day. I had been in a process of becoming. And that evening, I was going to leave all the pain – all the things I never wanted to be – right there in that water, and I was going to emerge a new person.

To prepare for my fresh start, I had to cut the final tie to what was becoming my old life: Derrick. Before I made the call, all morning I had been calling credit-card companies, removing his name from accounts, canceling his cards. Once he found out I was cutting him off, I didn't want to take the chance of him going on one last shopping spree and running up my credit cards.

My family's plane was due to arrive in 15 minutes. I couldn't put it off any longer. What would he say? What could he say? He had no say any more. This was my decision. God, give me the strength; give me the words, I pleaded silently.

I stared at the payphones lining the wall. A woman in a jogging suit leaning on her suitcase occupied the one in the middle. I would use the one on the far left. I can do all things. *I can do all things through Christ who gives me strength.* I walked to the phone with more confidence than I knew I had and fished for some coins in my wallet. Without hesitation, I dropped the change into the phone and dialed the number. The phone rang; and rang; and rang. Please pick up! Please, please pick up! I *have* to do this, I thought to myself.

'Hello?' His deep voice was slow and lingering; so unsuspecting.

I began to wonder if I could really go through with it.

'Hey, it's me...' I can and I will, I told myself.

'Yeah... what's up?' he said, with his usual 'What do you want?' kind of tone.

'I'm just calling to let you know that I can't have you in my life any more, and from now on I will no longer be supporting you financially.' I spoke with more confidence then I knew I had. 'It stops here. Please don't call me. Please don't try to get in touch with me.'

'What? I don't understand,' he stammered.

I knew the look on his face without seeing it. It was the *what-the-hell-is-wrong-with-you-have-you-lost-your-damn-mind* look.

'You don't have to understand. You just have to accept it. Please don't try to call me,' I replied calmly, as though I had rehearsed it a thousand times. In actuality the words just came to me.

'I have to go.' And with that I hung up the phone, and with it an era of my life. Steadily, I sat down and looked towards the gate to see if my aunt's and grandmother's plane had landed. It hadn't.

That's it. After seven years, a two-minute phone call was all it took to end it. And I am alive. The world has not stopped for this moment. Life goes on. My life will go on. Some days I had tried to imagine my life without Derrick. I had tried to picture the end of our relationship. I had always thought it would come by death – his or mine. And if he had died first, I would be sure to follow.

He was gone from me, and I was still very much alive. There was something else, too; a chain around my neck that needed to be removed. Long ago, Derrick had given me a rare gift: a gold rope necklace with a tiny gold cat, sitting delicately with its tail poised in an S-shape at its side. That unexpected thoughtfulness – he knew I loved cats – made it extra precious. The fact that he thought enough about me to pick out something that I liked was one of those small threads of kindness that I hung onto with all my might, hoping that they were an indication of some deeper measure of love for me that would one day surface. These tiny threads were still all I had. The tighter I held, the more they wound themselves around me and sliced their way into my skin.

I reached around to the clasp and struggled to open it. When I couldn't get my thumbnail to hold the lever long enough to unlatch the chain, I pulled the clasp around where I could see it. With my chin pressed against my chest, I finally forced it free. I noticed that there was an area of rough skin where the cat had been resting against my neck for all those years. Now my skin can finally breathe! Now I can finally breathe, I thought. I wanted to break all the chains that bound me to him.

I caught a glimpse of my grandmother's perfectly set, silvery-cotton hair through a crowd of people. Walking beside her, with her hurried pigeon-toed walk, was my Auntie Krissy. As they got closer, I could see by the looks on their faces they were growing impatient with the slowly meandering passengers blocking their path. Lollygagging was never their thing.

I waved to get their attention. Auntie Krissy spotted me first and made a beeline for me, with her arms outstretched. Her brown eyes were rimmed with tears, as though I hadn't just visited her in Phoenix two months before. She took me in her arms, and I caught the subtle smell of fabric softener and expensive perfume. Equally excited to see me, but more reserved in her expression, my grandmother stood waiting for her turn to hug me, while Auntie Krissy smushed my cheeks between her manicured hands.

'I'm so proud of you, baby,' my aunt gushed. She had been praying for this day for years. When I called to tell her I was being baptized, it was her idea that she and my grandmother fly out.

My grandmother's hug, strong yet quick, came standard with a firm series of pats on my back.

'Well, look at you! You cut that hair of yours. Now that looks smart,' my grandmother began her commentary on my appearance. 'It's not hanging down around your shoulders like a hippy any more.'

I smirked to myself, knowing what she would never know: the haircut had nothing to do with looking smart for Grandma, and everything to do with cutting off the past. How many customers had my long sandy-blonde strands of hair brushed across? How many times had I flirtatiously flung my hair around, letting it cascade over my naked body? She would never know. As I stood before my grandmother's adoring gaze, I finally felt like the person I always wanted her to think I was. I wouldn't have to pretend any more.

'Yeah, Grandma; I figured it was time for a change.'

I am standing barefoot in my light blue, breezy, cotton ankle-length dress. I lift my chin and look up – past the rafters and the skies above them – beyond. If I close my eyes, I can feel the warm, damp sand of the Jordan River beneath my feet. A wild, locust-eating man named John the Baptizer stands before me. The words of a prophet ring out into the warm air: 'I am the voice of one calling in the desert. Make straight the way for the Lord.' There is a gentle breeze on my neck, the fluttering wings of a dove. Eyes open, feet climbing the carpeted stairs leading to the tub of water, I know that God is with me. I know with everything inside me that my life was both unraveling and raveling at that very moment.

In the crowd I see my aunt's face. She is beaming: holding back tears, rejoicing in this moment. Yet she could never fully comprehend the weight of all I am taking with me into this pool; all I will leave behind. I am led into the tepid waters by the strong and tender hands of a man in a purple two-piece suit. The bottom of my dress becomes wet and heavy, gently guiding my descent. The pastor's smile is subtle and reverent; he is standing ready to lead me into this plunge of faith.

He prays for me, but his voice is distant. I am on top of a cumulus cloud, the face of my Love shining upon me. Then, all that I am and have been is covered. I am submerged in Him. Rising, only the best of me emerges. Arise, I am new! Today and every day.

I am standing before a cheering crowd, my family among them. Even my mother and Daddy Russ are celebrating for me, though my faith of choosing was hard for them to accept. No one is taking from me with their eyes. They aren't giving accolades for pole tricks or a perfect tan line. They are celebrating with me, for me.

On the night of my baptism I had a dream. It was a break from the violent re-occurrings where I am chasing and being chased by powerful creatures sent to destroy me; where I wake up tired from fighting with all my might, my weapons as puny as toothpicks. In this dream I was free and flying, inches above sparkling indigo waters brushed by winds into miles of tossing waves. Beneath me I saw the reflection of a kind face, compassionate and knowing. He is my Jesus. Swept up and carried across the vast unknown, I was filled with a peace I have never known, awake or asleep. I knew that He is with me.

Three months later, I had a new job; a new life. Five teenage girls sat at the table of a group home in South Central, eating cereal. The meager pay I received was worth the satisfaction of doing something meaningful with my life. At 22, I was no more than seven years older than most of them, and I looked nearly their age, but the owner of the home saw fit to hire me anyway.

The house we sat in was nestled on a hill above Crenshaw Boulevard. Neighbors passing by on their morning walks, armed with large sticks to fend off stray dogs, might think that this 1960s-style, swanky box house was like any other home in the neighborhood. They would not have known that inside this home with immaculate off-white carpets and rooms decorated to perfection resided the orphans of the living. These were the children of parents who were unable or unwilling to care for them as deemed fit by the government. Instead, they were shuffled from group home to group home, social worker to social worker.

When I first saw the home during my interview, I was struck by its cleanliness and beauty. *This is so much nicer than the group home I stayed in*, I thought to myself. But what the house had in spotlessness and fancy décor it lacked in warmth. If we wanted – if we had it in us – these girls and I could all pretend that we were one big happy family, living in this pristine house. But the girls had long since given up on admitting to the hope of family. And I was staff, a role that created a barrier between these girls and me. 'You don't care about us. You're only here for the money!' they tossed their accusations.

I wanted to tell them the truth: that no person in their right mind would work as the sole staff on the graveyard shift at a group home in South Central for $7 an hour if caring were not a part of the equation. Would it change their minds to know that in my previous line of work, I could make $1,000 working half the hours? Or that I could be working a low-stress job making twice the money, if I had been willing to get a little 'creative' and lie on my résumé? Some things were more important than money. That is what I had come to learn.

'Trust me: I am here because I want to be,' was all I could offer them. And they knew the rest of the story: that I too had lived in a group home and had always wanted to return as staff, to inspire someone else as I had been inspired by my favorite residential counselor. Somehow, I think my stint in the system did little to impress these long-timers. This wasn't a chapter in their lives; it was the only life they knew.

This wasn't home for them. And their precious hearts were far too broken by this time to allow them to play make-believe. They were just passing through. For all the porcelain vases and the dusting and vacuuming the girls did to keep the place spotless, under the surface it was still a Level 12 facility. Level 12 group homes were the last stop on the way to a lockdown facility. Most of the girls in them were just one 'incident' away from losing the last bit of freedom allotted to them, or one tantrum away from replacement.

Toya, a heavy-set girl with disheveled hair and wild eyes, glanced up from her cereal.

'Miss Harmony, what time is it?'

'It's 7.00 am. You have ten minutes until your bus arrives.'

She quickly stood up, and we walked over to the cabinet where her pills were kept. I unlocked the cabinet and pulled down a sufficient cocktail of medications to tranquilize a horse: Aderol for attention deficit disorder; Ativan for anxiety; Haldol for schizophrenia. The medications were more for the benefit of teachers and staff than for Toya. I put the Ativan back, and handed her the Haldol and Aderol.

'What about my Ativan, Miss Harmony?' The prescription was 'as needed', but Toya had become dependent on it.

'Toya, you don't need it.'

'I've been good. I haven't had an episode.'

'I know. That's why you don't need it. Plus it makes you so drowsy; how are you supposed to learn anything at school?'

The other staff had dished it out to her like candy. As long as she was drugged up, she wouldn't – or rather she couldn't – 'act up'. While she gulped down her pills, I noticed the buttons on her shirt were misbuttoned, so that one side of her shirt crept up and exposed her tummy.

'Toya, make sure you fix your buttons before you leave,' I whispered to her so the others wouldn't hear. Her eyes shot down and then back up at me, before she darted out of the room.

A few moments later, Toya whisked back into the kitchen, flung her backpack over her shoulder, and bounded out the door to catch the bus to her 'special school'. Karla and Diana, needing ample time to put on their make-up and fix their hair, had already left the table. Alexis and Aisha were still sitting there. Alexis, eyes glassy and tired, was staring into her bowl at the left-over milk. Aisha was pushing a few flakes of cereal around, postponing the ever-dreaded dish duty.

'OK, girls, we're leaving in ten minutes. And Aisha, you know it's your turn to do the dishes…' I noted.

Alexis and Aisha stayed sitting at the table, without looking up from their bowls. I could sense a battle of the wills forming. Not wanting to give them ammunition, I turned to the desk and began filling out the morning log. Thirty seconds passed, and they were still in a stalemate. I glanced up from my paperwork to see Alexis looking up from her bowl at Aisha. Alexis seemed to sense Aisha's resolve, and decided to back down. She pushed her chair away from the table and got up, leaving her bowl for Aisha to clean.

'All right, Aisha; let's go. I don't want you to be late for school,' I prompted her.

'I heard you the first time!' she yelled, slamming her bowl down hard. Small flakes of cereal popped out of her dish and splattered onto the table. Her nearly six-foot frame stood tall and firm, her eyes locked on me like a lion on her prey. I had well learned the art of de-escalation. When I was 17, my therapist and I would talk though all the possible outcomes of not reacting to anger and threats.

'You can't control what other people do. You can only control your reaction to them,' my therapist would say. And I came to find that she was right. Using her advice, I discovered something wonderful: *control*. I had control. It was a beautiful thing: to not let someone else's words and actions dictate mine; to rebel against scripted arguments and fits of raging.

As I stood in the kitchen across from Aisha, I noticed something new: my de-escalation technique of remaining calm did not require any restraint at all. There was no rage or pride to squelch. What I felt was something altogether different: compassion. I leaned against the kitchen counter, every muscle in my body free from tension. Aisha stood firm and upright. She seemed to be waiting for me to provoke her. Alexis and Karla came out of their rooms and assumed the role of bystanders.

'All right, girls. I need you to finish getting ready for school,' I coaxed Alexis and Karla.

Encouraged by the presence of an audience, Aisha took escalation into her own hands. As quick as a whip, she grabbed the gallon of milk that was sitting on the kitchen table and flung it at my head. It careered across the room and I ducked to miss the blow just in time. The jug hit the edge of the refrigerator, and milk gushed through the kitchen.

'I'll kill you! You hear me? I'll kill you!' she screamed, just before storming out of the room.

There was a part of me that wondered if she had it in her. Could she kill me? Would she? She was affiliated with the Bloods. And even though she went to a school dominated by a rival gang, the Crips, she still had the guts to sport red, her Blood regalia, among them. Past her anger, there was so much brokenness. She wouldn't hurt me. Her rage had nothing to do with me. I believe that she wanted to kill. But what she wanted to kill were the circumstances in her life. She had no control. Her mother's addiction; her father's incarceration; the lineage of violence that she was expected to be a part of: she didn't choose to join a gang because she thought it was cool. It was thrust upon her, like a family trade handed down through generations. Since she couldn't change the big things that determined the very course of her life, all she had were the small things, like whether or not she did the dishes.

In the past, my response to Aisha would have been altogether different. Her brokenness would have tapped into my brokenness. My instinct would have told me to prepare for battle. But something inside me had changed. Instead of restrained hurt and anger, I felt empathy. I saw Aisha through different eyes, and these new eyes mandated grace for her.

Karla and Alexis were still watching me from the corner of the room. Alexis went to get a roll of paper towels and began cleaning up the aftermath of Aisha's anger. Karla stood staring at me, with tears forming in her eyes.

'What's the matter, Karla?' I prompted.

'What is wrong with *you*, Harmony? Why the hell do you

love us so much?' She forced anger into her voice. She ran to her room and slammed the door.

On the drive to school that morning, my cramped little Honda, normally brimming with chatter and antics, was silent. Even Aisha sat still and calm, with her backpack on her lap, staring out the window watching the people on Crenshaw Boulevard: kids with backpacks walking to school; people at bus stops on their way to work; and the homeless man with dreadlocks down to his ankles wandering around Leimert Park. One by one, the girls trickled out of the car to their respective schools. Aisha was the last to be dropped off. She paused before opening her door, and looked at me with her round brown eyes.

'You gonna be there tonight?' she said, looking into her lap. She wanted a fresh start.

'Yep, I'll be there.' We all just want a fresh start.

'All right, then. See you later.'

'Have a good day.'

I watched Aisha, bold and tender, with her sweatshirt as red as a siren, part through a sea of other students wearing dim blue dickeys and royal blue jumpsuits. Yes, she was a fighter. It was all she knew.

On the drive home, I remembered Karla's words: 'Why the hell do you love us so much?'

I had never told the girls I loved them. As a staff member, that would have been unacceptable. But somehow Karla knew, and it was unsettling to her. I could understand her qualms. I saw myself in her. For so many years, true love – the kind of love that sees your flaws and embraces you anyway – was baffling to me. I was certain that if anyone really knew me they wouldn't like me, and they surely wouldn't love me. I did my best to hide behind a mask of sensuality, confidence, intellectualism, and all the things that I thought people approved of. I needed my mask as a soldier needs his weapon: to defend, to combat, to survive.

And God. If there really was a God, surely He was sitting high and mighty on His throne picking out all the good people, the ones worth loving, and thrusting disaster upon the bad ones, like me. I would never make the cut. Of that I was quite certain. The idea of anyone loving me – namely, God – was at best childish hope, nearing the absurdity of belief in Santa. Like me, Karla and Aisha had been taught by the harsh circumstances in their lives not to hope. It was the best way never to be disappointed.

What an audacious thing it was to hope! To believe in what you can't see with your eyes. And somehow, as the golden warmth of the sun poured into my car and cut the morning chill, illuminating people and trees and me, I knew that hope was all that I had. It was enough.

For years I longed for security, desiring to find it in tangible things. If I had enough money, I would feel safe. If I had the approval of men, I would feel wanted. But as I drove down Crenshaw Boulevard towards the 10 Freeway, none of that mattered the way it used to.

I had less money than I had had in years. There had been no man to prove myself to for nearly six months. Yet there was a Love pouring into me, penetrating my anger and hurt and doubt and fears: replacing them, in fact, with compassion, healing, hope and courage. In that moment, I felt a sense of contentment I had never known before, and it occurred to me that I would be OK. *I am going to be OK. I am OK.* Without the man and the money and all of my old security blankets, I would be OK.

The fullness of this realization bubbled up in me so fiercely that I had to keep myself from jumping out of the car and telling the homeless man on the corner that he would be OK too. Second chances are for real; people really do change; and there is a Love that sees to it all.

I am not who I was. I am not even who I was yesterday. Tomorrow I will be new again, and again, until I am completely the woman I was meant to be. Still, in this moment, in this breath that I am taking, I am enough. Right now – as is – I am worth loving and fighting for. This God of mine has shown me that. He is enough.

My heart danced in my chest. *He is enough.* The world around me shifted, and there was hope in every person I saw, connecting me to them in a way I had never noticed. The woman using her rear-view mirror to put on lipstick; the man standing on the center divider selling incense; the child with its forehead pressed up against the back-seat window; the young woman in hot pink stretch pants, walking rapidly, searching frantically for her next fix. *He is enough.*

And if He is all I ever have…

He is enough. And I am enough in Him.

EPILOGUE

The night I put those postcards on the windshields outside the strip club, I had no idea of the scale of God's plan. It seemed a simple thing – the only thing I could do at that moment.

The following week, I told Jeff, an associate pastor at my church, about what I had done. He was the first person at church besides Tanya who knew about my job at the strip club, and he had always accepted me. Still, I was half worried that he was going to tell me that Christians weren't supposed to go to strip clubs.

Instead, his eyes got big and he threw his arms around me. Then, as I ranted on about how I thought it would be great to start visiting the clubs regularly, and how I hoped to get other girls involved, he was practically finishing my sentences.

'When are you going to start?' he asked enthusiastically.

Up to that point it had been all dreams and ideas. I hadn't actually planned on *starting* the thing quite yet.

'Well, I don't know. I just started grad school and my plate is pretty full. It might be a while before I can commit to it…' I began offering excuses. As excited as I was about the prospect of starting a strip-club outreach, I had never heard of such a thing. There was no prototype that I knew of, and the thought of actually doing it was just short of terrifying.

'OK, Harmony.' He seemed to ponder my dilemma. 'How 'bout December?' It was now October. Jeff wasn't hearing my excuses. It seemed he knew that all I needed was a little encouragement in the form of a fire under my behind, because the next thing I knew, he had written up a blurb in our church bulletin about Treasures, the new strip-club outreach at Oasis.

In December 2003, I waited anxiously at the first meeting, wondering if anyone would actually show up. They did. About half a dozen women who seemed almost as nervous as I was arrived for the meeting. I brought a vision statement, the same one we use today, and a route of clubs for us to visit the following month to the meeting. In all honesty, I was pretty clueless, and the volunteer training was about as extensive as this: 'OK, girls, I am not really sure what to expect. This is going to be a work in progress. Are you with me? Now let's pray!' The only thing I really knew was that there was a mandate in my heart for us to show up. So that is what we did.

Back then, we didn't have a budget for gift bags or anything fancy like that. Our greatest assets were passion, a friend who did web design, and access to the printer at church. I wanted to communicate God's love without sounding preachy, so I figured the best way to do that was to tell my story. People can argue Scripture and doctrine till they're blue in the face, but nobody can argue with personal experience. So I poured out my heart on a page, had a few hundred copies printed up, and we planned to bring them to the clubs, hoping to leave them on the cars of the girls that worked there.

The following month, on the night of our first outreach, it started to rain. Quietly leaving our little pamphlets on windshields didn't seem like such a great idea after all. We were going to have to do this the hard way. We pulled up to the bizarrely named Jumbo's Clown Room, a small but well-known Hollywood strip club. My heart was pounding fiercely as we approached the club. The door was unmanned: no bouncer, no security. So we walked into the club with as much confidence as we could muster. The moment we set foot inside, the blaring music stopped suddenly, and all the people in the club seemed to look directly at us. Even the girl on stage stopped dancing and stood watching us, holding onto the pole as if someone had pressed the pause button on her routine. We all stood frozen, too, as if time had stopped for just a moment. Within seconds, the music resumed and everyone carried on about their business. To this day, I don't really know what happened that night in Jumbo's Clown Room. It could have been a coincidence that the entire club stopped in its tracks when we arrived on the scene. Regardless, this was the grandest entrance into strip-club outreach we could have imagined.

We finally found the manager at the back of the club, and did our best to act calm and professional.

'Um… We are a support group for women in the business. Some of us have worked in it ourselves. We just wanted to leave these pamphlets for your girls,' I said, trying not to stutter and stammer. To our delight, he took the pamphlets and assured us he would give them to the dancers. After the outreach that night, I was so filled with excitement and adrenaline, I couldn't sleep for hours. I finally felt as though all of the pain I had experienced throughout my life had been given a purpose.

For the next several months, we did the same thing at clubs throughout the city, all the while praying that the managers wouldn't simply trash the pamphlets once we had left. Our assurance rested in website hits, which spiked after every outreach.

The following Valentine's Day, we decided we would do something special for the girls. We made them little pink gift bags filled with lip gloss, earrings, sample-size perfumes, and anything else we could get our hands on. When we showed up at the clubs, we were floored by the response. Rather than simply taking our gift bags and sending us on our way, they began inviting us into the clubs to personally deliver the gifts to the girls. The Bible says, 'Your gift will make a way for you.' In the case of our outreach, it was very true. For the first time we were able to connect with the women face to face in the clubs. When the girls asked why we were giving them something for free, we told them: 'Because we want you to know that you are loved!'

Today, there are over 30 women on the Treasures team. Together, they visit 170 strip clubs annually and reach thousands of women with gift bags filled with cosmetics, jewelry and the simple message that they are loved and valued. Many women throw their arms around us and thank us profusely for what seems like such a simple gesture. Others are shocked that someone would give them something with no strings attached: not knowing how to receive this, they offer to pay us for the gifts.

The outreaches are the fun part. Getting together with friends and doling out lip gloss and earrings to God's beloved daughters, who wouldn't have a good time? It's what happens after the outreach is over that tugs at my heart and sends me to my knees. It's when the women contact us and share their stories that we see the painful reality that many face. A woman with children to support, no education and no job experience, desperate to leave the industry. A girl who was drugged, raped and forced into prostitution and pornography. A girl who started stripping to pay for cancer treatments. Another who found herself on the streets at the age of 15; selling her body was the only way she knew how to survive. And the girl who made her way out of the sex industry, but finds herself facing shame, depression, anxiety and emotional scars from the years she spent in it.

Treasures, now an official non-profit organization, offers

prayer and support to these women in the form of encouragement, resources, referrals and peer mentoring. Our desire is to equip women working in all areas of the sex industry, and those who have left it behind, to live the healthy, flourishing lives they were created to live. We believe that transformation begins at a heart level, and are passionate about seeing hearts revolutionized by the love and grace of God.

Melanie Star is a young woman who embodies this vision. After hearing about Treasures, Melanie was so moved she asked if she could come with us on an outreach, even though she wasn't ready to give up her job at the strip club. One night with the team was all it took before she announced that she was going to clean out her locker at work and leave stripping behind. Not because we told her to, or made her feel bad about what she did for a living, but because God was doing a work inside her. It's not our job to judge and convict people. All we have to do is love people and trust in God and His goodness, because it's the goodness of God that inspires people to change. That is exactly what Melanie did. She continued volunteering with Treasures while she finished school. Today she lives in Nebraska, where she works as a property manager for a multi-family housing development. She boldly shares her story to reach and encourage other women, and continues to support the work of Treasures through prayer and financial partnership.

Today there are more women working in the sex industry than at any other time in history. In the United States alone there are more than 2,700 strip clubs, more than in any nation in the world. A big job for a grassroots, Los-Angeles-based organization. While we continue to work with women all over the country, we know that we can accomplish more, through training and equipping other passionate leaders to run outreaches with the support of their local churches. To date, there are strip-club outreaches using the Treasures model in 11 states.

God never wastes a hurt. I truly believe that, if we let him, God will use everything we have been through for good. We all have a story to tell.

This has been an account of my exodus: my journey out of captivity. It is by no means the entire story, as it hasn't ended yet. Today I am freer and more fulfilled than I was yesterday. Tomorrow, I believe I will be freer still. The journey is ongoing. I am not perfect, but I am complete. I have a beautiful daughter, amazing friends, an education, and I get to spend my days reaching and loving women in the sex industry and sharing hope with them. I am complete not because of the circumstances in my life, but because of Who I am living for. I have learned that faith is the substance of things hoped for, and the evidence of things unseen (Hebrews 11:1). There have been plenty of times when I have had to summon this faith, a faith that lives outside of facts and reason.

The road has been long and often challenging. Transformation did not magically happen overnight. Nearly 11 years have passed since the day I left the strip club. And just as the scars that formed throughout the early part of my life happened by a process of ongoing abrasion, so the healing of them has been a process. It took many years to arrive at a place where my self-esteem was so low that I was willing to sell my body in order to support an abusive and unfaithful boyfriend just to avoid being alone. For so long, I thought that leaving him would be futile, because I believed that any other man on the planet would treat me just as poorly. As we so often do, I stayed in my dysfunction because it was most familiar to me, and familiarity was the closest thing to comfort I knew. Emerging from that has taken time, and it's an ongoing process.

So this portion of my story ends with a revelation: that I am enough. That God is enough. And every revelation I have had, every choice I have made since that point, has been laid on that foundation. Were I to end with a tale of happily ever after, I would undermine the journey itself.

Before I even thought about getting into another relationship, I first had to learn to be alone with God. I spent time getting to know Him and getting to know myself. Jesus healed my heart, but the transformation and renewing of my mind was a process, requiring action and commitment on my part. I had to replace old ways of thinking with new ones; lies with the truth. And when I found that painful memories and the wounds that accompanied them did not magically disappear, I enlisted the prayers and listening ears of my friends and sought the help of a Christian therapist. I needed to do everything I could to pursue the healing and restoration that was available to me.

The people in my life have stood by my side and loved me unconditionally, but none of them rescued me from my former life. Only God could do that. And as important as my relationships are, I know that there will always be deep needs innate in me that only God can meet. My friends did not heal the hurts in my heart, though they have held my hand and their T-shirts have been wet with my tears. My Master's degree and the knowledge that came with it did not fix me. People and things have enriched me, but they do not define me.

This brings me to God, who loved me while I was still in the middle of my deepest mess. My relationship with Him did not begin once I 'got my act together'. He not only loves us in spite of our junk, but He sees past all of it to the person He has created us to be. God loved me just as much standing half-naked in the middle of a strip club as He does today. I didn't somehow gain His approval by doing or saying the right things. I didn't need to win His heart. He won mine.

> BUT ALL I SEE LOOKS BACK AT ME LOVED BY SOMEONE. AND THE GOLDEN THREAD OF THE NATURE OF ALL THIS IS SIMPLY THAT WE ARE A PART OF EVERYTHING THAT WILL EVER EXIST. TO BE LOVED BY SOMEONE IS WHY WE'VE COME.

Rickie Lee Jones

A LAST WORD

On the eleventh anniversary of my leaving the sex industry we had one of the most memorable outreaches EVER.

For starters, we had a young woman go out on her very first outreach since escaping the traffickers who brutally forced her into sex work. We had been walking alongside her for the previous couple of years and that night she was ready to turn her pain into purpose. She was so thankful for the healing and rebuilding that had taken place in her life that she wept with gratitude throughout the night. It was an honor to witness this moment in her journey.

At the end of the evening we pulled up to the strip club where I used to work. This club was a landmark in so many ways. It was the place where, as a broken nineteen-year old girl, I first stripped and sold myself to strangers. It was also the place where, years later, a compassionate manager, who felt just as trapped as I did, offered to pray with me that God would help me find a way out of the club. Weeks later, God clearly spoke a message to my heart that gave me the strength to leave: 'I am going to take care of you. I will never let you down.' And He hasn't. This was also the club where I sat outside, wondering if there was any way I could reach the girls still working there, my heart bleeding with prayers, remembering them. As it turns out, there was a way – and a simple message, 'Her value is far above rubies and pearls.'

That night, on the eleventh anniversary of the weekend I quit, and after six and a half years of visiting that very club, desiring to speak love, value and purpose into the lives of the women working there, we were told that the club would be closing the following day. After fifty-three years of business, the building would be levelled and turned into an airport parking lot. This would be my last time at the club. And while many of the clubs we visit allow us to hand-deliver the gift bags to the girls, this particular club always received them at the door and never allowed us inside.

Something in me would not let me leave. So I asked the manager if he would let us in, just so that I could say a proper 'goodbye'.

And for the first time since we have been doing outreach, I walked into the club. It felt as though I had entered a time warp. Aside from some wooden stalls they had built for extra private lap dances, nothing had changed. Even many of the staff were the same. Some of them said that they were happy the club was closing – that they finally had a reason to leave the industry. One woman who had been there twenty-five years said that she would have died in that club if it wasn't shutting down! Others were not as glad to hear the news. They didn't know where or whether they would be able to find work. We were able to tell them about some of the resources we have.

As I walked in, a young woman threw her arms around me saying, 'I have always wanted to meet the girls who have been bringing us gifts. For six years we have looked forward to these gifts. Nobody EVER gave us anything or did anything nice for us. You were the only ones who cared.' She brought out her camera to take pictures with us and cried like we were long lost sisters.

We spent some time in the dressing room, talking to the girls about their plans for the future. It was the same dressing room where, piece by piece, I sold my outfits on the night I quit, knowing there was no turning back. These women too are at such a pivotal moment in their lives and we hope they will take us up on our offer of support. Where many clubs have high turnover rates, this particular club seems to have kept the employees they hire. Many of the girls reported that this was the first and only club they had ever worked at. And after several years, it was all they knew.

One woman told a volunteer, 'This is the only home I have ever known…and there's no place like home.'

This statement struck me because I can remember a time when the strip club was the only home I knew. I can remember a time when I had become so familiar with being sexualized and objectified that it was comfortable to me. So comfortable, it was almost comforting.

And 'home' is exactly what I found on the day I walked into the Oasis, my church. 'I am finally home' were the words that came to my heart. I could feel my Loving Father, with His hands outstretched, welcoming me.

We hope and pray that each of these women will discover a home – a refuge – unlike any they have known. And that the closing of this club will mark a new beginning in their lives. That they will come to know that they are loved, valued and purposed and that this revelation will penetrate every corner of their hearts and lives! Here's to new beginnings!

MY HEALING JOURNEY

Every journey is different. Every time Jesus healed someone in the Bible, He did it differently. And so it is with us. There is no secret formula for healing, but I believe that there are steps that we can take and choices we can make that will give strength to our lives. Here are just a few of the things that I discovered on my own healing journey.

Relate

There is no substitute for a real and honest relationship with God. He is Lord over my life and so much more. Through reading His word, praying and simply spending time being quiet and still with Him, I have come to know Him as Father, Friend, Comforter, Healer, Redeemer, Provider, and the Lover of my soul. He is not a distant God, sitting in some far-off place judging you and me. He is a God of mercy, grace and compassion. He is Immanuel, God who is with us.

Plant

We are not meant to do life alone. Humans are relational beings, designed for community. A tree cannot grow unless it is planted, and I strongly believe that my life would not bear the fruit it has if I had not been planted in my church. I am not talking about simply doing the Christian duty of sitting through a Sunday service. I believe that the local church plays an irreplaceable role on this planet. When the local church is healthy, it is a place where people can come to worship, learn, grow, and experience healing, grace, mercy, and the unconditional love of God. It is where I have built some of my most meaningful and flourishing relationships, with people who know me – imperfections and all – and love me anyway.

Decide

In the Bible (John 5), we read the story of a man, lying on a mat, who had been disabled for 38 years. Jesus asks him a question: 'Do you want to get well?' At that point, the man starts coming up with excuses, saying that nobody would help him, and every time he tried to get better, somebody got in his way. Ultimately, Jesus instructs the man to 'Take up his mat and walk.' He follows this instruction and is healed.

I believe that Jesus is asking you and me the same question: do you want to get well? Sometimes we think we want to get better, but when it comes down to it, we have a million excuses as to why we can't. We become comfortable with our condition, and content to remain paralyzed on our mats.

Ultimately, the decision is in our hands. Nobody can want it for us. God can't force it on us. We must decide to get well.

Replace

Eleven years ago, I believed a lot of lies. They were so woven into the fabric of my being that they became my personal truth. I believed that I was worthless, stupid, and unlovable. My life reflected what I thought to be true, because I made choices based on those deep and hidden beliefs.

The Bible tells us to 'Be transformed by the renewing of your mind' (Romans 12:2). It also says that we are to 'take captive every thought to make it obedient to Christ' (2 Corinthians 10:5).

There is a process of transformation that requires action on our part. It is up to us to actively replace the lies we believe with the truth.

Face

In the well-known story of David and Goliath, David faced and defeated his giant with a sling and a stone. Historically, in the days of Exodus, the Israelites had been afraid to enter the promised land because of the many 'giants' who inhabited that territory. It was the fear of the giants, not the giants themselves, that kept the people from God's promise for them.

In my own journey, I have had to face some big giants: sexual abuse, rape, father issues, fear, rejection, abandonment, unforgiveness, and bitterness, to name a few. To rattle them off in a list like this is easy, but to actually face each of these head-on has been a battle. I can distinctly remember fighting though Los Angeles traffic to make the one-and-a-half-hour commute to see my therapist, where I had to pay upwards of $60 an hour to face some of my giants. I would much rather have been sitting on my couch, eating chocolate ice cream and watching reruns of Seinfeld. But if I wanted to walk in the fullness of God's promises for my life, there were giants to be faced. Sometimes I felt like David: as if I was facing a seasoned combatant with weapons as puny as a sling and a stone. But during those times I learned that, like David, God has given me the tools I need to face the giants in my life, and that I never have to face them on my own.

Forgive

I used to think that some things were simply unforgivable, rape and murder among them. I felt completely justified in hating the ex-boyfriend who raped me. To forgive him seemed to mean that what he did was OK, and it wasn't.

Eventually, I learned that forgiveness is a vertical transaction between me and God, not a horizontal one between me and another human. God has forgiven me and He asks me to forgive others.

I have heard it said that forgiveness is setting someone free, and realizing the prisoner was you. At first I forgave out of obedience; but when I finally forgave, I realized that I was the one being held captive by my unforgiveness. The people that had hurt me were living their lives, going about their merry way, while I was seething with anger, hurt and bitterness. Unforgiveness was holding *me* prisoner.

Stay

The journey is never over, so be gracious with yourself and stay committed to the course. We are all in a process of becoming: becoming healed, becoming whole, becoming closer to God, and becoming all that we are created to be.

God is a gentleman. He never forces us to change or gives us more than we can bear. He walks us through this process one step at a time. In His strength, we are able to face our giants one by one.

I could apply 110 steps to healing and read a zillion self-help books, but what I am able to accomplish on my own pales in comparison with what can happen when I invite the transforming, gracious and redeeming power of God into my life. His love transcends knowledge, reason, and human effort.

> *And I pray that you, being rooted and established in love, may have power, together with all the saints, to grasp how wide and long and high and deep is the love of Christ, and to know this love that surpasses knowledge – that you may be filled to the measure of all the fullness of God.*
>
> *Now to him who is able to do immeasurably more than all we ask or imagine, according to his power that is at work within us, to him be glory in the church and in Christ Jesus throughout all generations, for ever and ever! Amen.*
>
> *Ephesians 3:17–21*

REPLACING THE LIES

The Truth About a Treasure

She is Valued

She is far more precious than jewels, and her value is
far above rubies or pearls.

Proverbs 31:10, Amplified Bible

How precious to me are your thoughts, O God!
How vast is the sum of them!
Were I to count them,
they would outnumber the grains of sand.

Psalm 139:17–18

She is Loved

'Though the mountains be shaken
and the hills be removed,
yet my unfailing love for you will not be shaken
nor my covenant of peace be removed,'
says the Lord, who has compassion on you.

Isaiah 54:10

The Lord appeared to us in the past, saying:
'I have loved you with an everlasting love;
I have drawn you with loving-kindness.'

Jeremiah 31:3

Neither height nor depth, nor anything else in all
creation, will be able to separate us from the love of
God that is in Christ Jesus our Lord.

Romans 8:39

She is Purposed

'For I know the plans I have for you,' declares the
Lord, 'plans to prosper you and not to harm you,
plans to give you hope and a future.'

Jeremiah 29:11

The Lord will fulfill his purpose for me;
    your love, O LORD, endures forever –
    do not abandon the works of your hands.

Psalm 138:8

She is Beautiful

The king is enthralled by your beauty;
    honor him, for he is your lord.

Psalm 45:11

I praise you because I am fearfully and wonderfully
    made;
    your works are wonderful, I know that full well.

Psalm 139:14

She is Redeemed

Therefore, if anyone is in Christ, (s)he is a new
creation; the old has gone, the new has come!

2 Corinthians 5:17

The Truth About God

He is Loving

His love endures forever.

Psalm 136:2

I have loved you with an everlasting love;
I have drawn you with loving-kindness.

Jeremiah 31:3

He is Faithful

Know therefore that the Lord your God is God; he is the faithful God, keeping his covenant of love to a thousand generations of those who love him and keep his commands.

Deuteronomy 7:9

The Lord himself goes before you and will be with you; he will never leave you nor forsake you. Do not be afraid; do not be discouraged.

Deuteronomy 31:8

He is Gracious

God is all mercy and grace –
not quick to anger, is rich in love.

Psalm 145:8, The Message

My grace is sufficient for you, for my power is made perfect in weakness.

2 Corinthians 12:9

He is Mighty

God is our refuge and strength,
  an ever-present help in trouble.
Therefore we will not fear, though the earth give way
  and the mountains fall into the heart of the sea,
though its waters roar and foam
  and the mountains quake with their surging.

Psalm 46:1–3

He is Caring

The Lord is close to the brokenhearted
  and saves those who are crushed.

Psalm 34:18

He is Comforting

As a mother comforts her child,
  so will I comfort you.

Isaiah 66:13

And God will wipe every last tear from their eyes.

Revelation 7:17, The Message

The Lord is close to the brokenhearted,
and saves those who are crushed.

Psalm 34:18

He is Near

The Lord is near to all who call on him,
  to all who call on him in truth.

Psalm 145:18

Speak it until you believe it!

THE STILETTO PROJECT

If this book has made an impact on you, and you are interested in partnering with us to make it available on a larger scale, here are some ideas on how you can be part of the Stiletto Project.

Spread the Word

Word of mouth is one of the most powerful and effective tools by which a book like this can develop a mainstream presence. Talk to people about *Scars and Stilettos* and the effect it has had on you.

If you have a website or a blog, write about how you have been personally touched by this book, and what it means to you.

Write a book review for your favorite magazine, website or newspaper.

If you own or manage a bookstore, consider displaying this book on your counter, or in your window display.

Share

Give this book to your friends and family, and people you believe would be impacted by this story. Many of those who have never been a part of the sex industry can relate to living in a way that does not reflect a person's true value, or to searching for significance in other people rather than God.

Purchase copies as a gift for women's residential programs, shelters, prisons, ministries, or any other program where people might be encouraged by a story of hope and redemption.

About Treasures

Treasures is a unique, faith-based outreach and support group for women in the sex industry, including victims of commercialized sexual exploitation and trafficking. As the only organization of its kind based in the adult industry capital of the world (San Fernando Valley in Los Angeles County) and one of the few survivor-led organizations in the country, our mission is to reach, restore and equip women in order to help them live healthy, flourishing lives.

Through Treasures Trainings, we are committed to train, equip and mobilize other churches and leaders to develop sex industry outreach leaders in 70 cities on 4 continents. Our goal is to see flourishing outreaches developed in every major city on the planet. See the website at www.iamatreasure.com.

Some Statistics

- More women are employed by the sex industry than at any other time in history.
- Between 66 and 90 per cent of women in the sex industry were sexually abused as children.
- Compared with the general population, women in the sex industry experience higher rates of substance abuse issues, rape and violent assault, sexually transmitted diseases, domestic violence, depression, and post-traumatic stress disorder.
- The women in this industry face many issues that affect their physical, emotional, and spiritual well-being. They are a largely unreached population, and many feel desperately isolated and alone. Even those who would contemplate going to church wonder if there truly is a place for them there. Will they find the restoration they are seeking in the house of God?
- Treasures is the first and only organization of its kind in the Los Angeles area.

How You Can Help

- Join the Treasures Prayer Team (Worldwide)
- Make a one-time financial contribution
- Become a Treasure Builder through monthly financial partnership
- Volunteer on the Treasures Outreach Team (Los Angeles, CA) or on one of our Treasures trained outreaches.
- Donate gifts in kind, such as cosmetics and jewelry, for our gift bags
- Invite Harmony to speak at your church or organization
- Attend a Treasures Sex Industry Outreach and Care Training to learn more about reaching women in your city. www.iamatreasure.com/gettrained

For more information on these and other opportunities, please visit www.iamatreasure.com

Donations can be made online or mailed to:
Treasures Ministries
PO # 5311
Sherman Oaks, CA 91413

Also Available

X Girls DVD Series and Workbook Curriculum
The X Girls series covers topics ranging from Boundaries to Sex and Dating, to dealing with the Aftermath of Sex Work. Questions from viewers are answered from the perspective of an ex-stripper, an ex-porn star, and an ex-prostitute. The workbook curriculum contains teaching content, discussion questions and workshop ideas and was designed to help sex industry outreach leaders and churches facilitate 10-week support/connect group sessions for the women they serve. It can also be done on an individual basis.

Stiletto Project: My Story Matters
Story matters. The Stiletto Project is Treasures' campaign to humanize the woman on the other end of the dollar through the use of story. Story reveals the brokenness that lies behind the sex industry's façade of glamour. Story illustrates the capacity to overcome. Her triumph demonstrates what is possible in our own lives when we engage Jesus. She is your daughter, your friend, your sister, your wife... maybe she is you. *Stiletto Project: My Story Matters* is a compilation of her stories.

All proceeds from these products support the work of Treasures.